HOW TO SURVIVE AND THRIVE

As a Newly Qualified Osteopath

Elizabeth Curphey

First Edition

May 2021

Copyright © 2021 Elizabeth Curphey

The author has asserted her rights under Section 77 of the Copyright, Designs and Patents Act, 1988, to be identified as the author of the work. All rights reserved. No portion of this book may be reproduced or transmitted in any form or by any means, electronic or mechanical, including photocopying and recording, or by any information storage and retrieval system, without permission in writing from the author.

CONTENTS

Foreword v

Welcome! vii

Why you need this book ix

Why did you choose to become an osteopath? 1

Where do I start? 7

The realities of life as an osteopath 23

Day to day practice life 31

How to build and sustain your business without
    burning out 49

Are you up to the job? 61

How to talk to patients in their own language 67

How to deal with 'difficult' patients 77

The magic is in the relationship – developing a deeper
    understanding of working as an osteopath 89

Creating a healthy relationship between principal
      and associate.............................. 93
Different values/ do you see eye to eye?........... 107
The boring but necessary bits.................... 115
Final words..................................... 125
References 127
About the author............................... 129

DEDICATION

To all those osteopaths who have gone before me, those who have forged a path in osteopathy, who taught me, guided me, employed me, helped me and nurtured me – thank you.

FOREWORD

This book is a 'must have' guide for all new graduates of Osteopathy, if not most manual therapies.

During these challenging times, I've noticed how many new graduates are feeling a little overwhelmed or unsure about their first steps into their new world of work.

Some may want to get some good quality mentoring and 'learning on the job' whilst others might be keen to open their own practice and crack on!

Either way, this book is an essential friend on your bookshelf which will guide you gently towards the goals you have decided upon.

Elizabeth has worked with me twice to further grow and expand her multi-disciplinary practice.

She is a confident practitioner, with a very down to earth and pragmatic approach to both her work and her life. This book is another example of her straightforward and no fluff advice for new graduates.

Together we have explored the issues that undergraduates are concerned about and Elizabeth has combined this information with her own experience to create this much needed reference book.

Using examples and stories, Elizabeth shares how to avoid the trip wires you may face and the mistakes you might make.

And she leads you confidently towards the triumphs of real practice life, whether you choose to be an associate or to set up by yourself.

Quite simply, this book prepares you for the successful career you dreamed of when you signed up to be an Osteopath.

Every new graduate should read this!

Gilly Woodhouse
Osteobiz Business Development Coach

WELCOME!

Firstly may I say a huge thank you for buying this book, whether the kindle version or the actual paper copy. You have made a great investment in helping yourself to become the best osteopath you can be.

This book is written from the heart, and with over 20 years of osteopathic experience. I'm not the only one who has had input in this book – all those I have learned from, watched in practice, worked for and whose books I have read have helped to shape me as an osteopath, and therefore this book. I am eternally grateful for all the guidance and knowledge I have received from my peers over my years in practice, and I hope that you will also learn from our combined experiences.

I also sincerely hope that you enjoy reading this book and that you will come back to it again and again as you develop as an osteopath and hone your skill set.

So without further ado – let's begin!

WHY YOU NEED THIS BOOK

When you finish your osteopathy training you are fully equipped to treat patients and help restore them back to mobility and health.

What you do not learn, however, is the whole act of running a business, knowing what procedures and policies to put in place, how to run an effective, efficient practice with the time you have available and how to manage other osteopaths and practitioners. Nor are you taught how to deal with difficult patients, colleagues and how to develop your own career and keep a healthy work-life balance.

During my time running my own thriving practice, I have picked up and learnt a lot of invaluable information and experience. I wrote this book to help other osteopaths carve out their career in the profession. It is the book I wish I could have read when I started out.

Osteopaths are unique

When I set up my own practice I made sure I consulted a lot of books about how to run a business. They were written by very experienced and knowledgeable business coaches, accountants and specialists, but not one had actually been an osteopath and experienced the challenges that we face.

It is true that some of the core elements of running any business apply to setting up your own practice. You do need to have a business plan, know your market and know how to grow your business to become more successful. However, what I noticed in reading these books was that none of them really understood my profession, what it was actually like to have a career as an osteopath. I know as a profession we like to think we are different, and I do actually believe that we do things in a different way from other businesses. One of our major downfalls however is that we are often not good business people. This book is for anyone who wants to run a successful osteopathic business while making sure they meet the needs of their patients at the same time.

Who should read this book?

This book is mostly aimed at newly qualified osteopaths, or NQO's as I will refer to them in the book. These are osteopaths who have been qualified less than five years, but if you have been qualified longer than that I am confident that you will find many useful hints and tips too!

Many NQOs feel quite unsupported when they first qualify. It is a big step going from a lovely supportive university clinic environment where you have tutors and friends on hand to help you, to working in a new environment, sometimes on your own depending upon your circumstances, where you will be faced with patients' problems and situations which you may never have encountered before.

It can be daunting. Where do I start? What is the best way to progress my career? How do I deal with finances and setting up a practice? There are many and varied questions when you first start out.

In writing this book I have also asked for contributions from other osteopathic colleagues and friends. Many of our experiences are similar, but it is always useful to get perspective from other sources. This way, I have combined the best tips from some of the most experienced practitioners in the country. Think of us as offering you friendly advice as you head off on your exciting new career as an osteopath.

In order to help you get the most out of this book I have divided it into sections which can be read independently of other sections. I've called these sections:

- Being an Osteopath
- The Practicalities
- The Boring but Necessary bits

You can either read this book cover to cover (and I hope you will!), or you can dip into whichever section you feel will be most helpful for you at that particular time.

In order for you to get even more value from this book you will notice as you go through that there are icons in the margins and these icons are there to identify different sections further. These icons are:

Insights

Real Life Examples

Advice

Further reading

Self-Reflection

Templates/Checklists

There are also resources available at:
www.thetherapyrooms.co.uk. > > Survive & Thrive menu > > Enter password S&T2021#New

WHY DID YOU CHOOSE TO BECOME AN OSTEOPATH?

This is probably one of the questions that I have been asked the most in my years of being an osteopath. I have a great answer for this, which involves ex-boyfriends, Hong Kong and law degrees but more of that later!

The 'WHY' is probably the most important we can ask ourselves about anything we want to achieve. If we have real clarity on why we want to do something, the 'how' will easily follow. In your wobbly moments in practice, which believe me you will have from time to time, the answer to this will help you to think about how to get through those tricky times. It will help you focus on the positive aspects of your decision making and give you clarity.

It might be a question which you haven't thought about in a while, maybe not since you started your training. It is such a great question to reflect back on though, as it helps you to focus on your reasons for being where you are now, what drew you to the profession in the first place and why you chose to spend all that money on getting your osteopathic degree.

Your answer may also help you to think about what kind of an osteopath you want to be. As a profession we are hugely diverse, with some people working on their own for their entire careers, some working in large practices with lots of osteopaths, and others being part of a multidisciplinary team. Some osteopaths are purely structural, others just use cranial techniques, some combine the two. Some osteopaths decide to specialise in one area or one speciality – I for example have a particular interest in babies and children and completed the diploma at the Osteopathic Centre for Children. Others like the diversity of treating whatever/whoever walks through their door. There are those that go into teaching, research or take up roles in the GOsC or IO. But hopefully we all have as a goal helping our patients to get out of pain and back to better health.

It's never too early to think about where you might want your osteopathic career to take you. I suggest that you take some time to ponder this question and, in the space, below write down a few thoughts as to the answer. This will be useful to come back to later and see if how you are working aligns with your reasons for choosing to work as an osteopath in the first place.

Why I became an osteopath

*

*

*

What makes a 'good osteopath'?

I thought the most helpful way to start this book would be for us to ponder this question.

During my research and planning for this book I asked my colleagues this question and was very interested in the replies. One point to ponder before you read the answers is what do I mean by a 'good osteopath'? Good for whom – patients, the osteopathic community, colleagues? For many experienced osteopaths being 'good' is less about how high you scored in your exam, it is thinking more about your overall behaviour, demeanour and professionalism.

Many of us in the profession believe that osteopaths are unique in the health care field. We believe that our view of healthcare, how the body works, and how we as healthcare professionals help the people who come to us is individual and holistic. There is some fear in those who have been qualified a long time that the essence of osteopathy, what A T Still discovered, believed and practiced, has been watered down in the current training.

So, I would implore you to read the work of AT Still to get a real understanding of where osteopathy came from. By holding his principals in high regard, it does not mean that you can't be a modern thinking osteopath. It means you have the advantage of being able to practice osteopathic medicine with all the advantages of the modern medical world, while still realising that the bodies you are working on are fundamentally the same as the bodies AT Still was working on. Check out the reference section at the end for more reading material on this subject.

As you read the statements below, you will see there are some common themes, about understanding, feeling and behaviours. Please don't panic if you don't believe you have all these skills yet; you are just starting out in your career and you will pick up a lot of these as you develop and progress as an osteopath.

What makes a 'Good Osteopath'?

- An inquiring mind
- A listening mind
- Good at problem-solving
- Taking a global, non-reductionist approach to patient care
- Caring, compassionate, patient-centred
- Honest and kind
- Having excellent communication skills
- Being able to multitask
- Having humility and integrity
- Have the ability to reflect on your practice and yourself
- Being resilient and having lots of energy
- Having an invisible armour

- Being non judgemental
- Having a good combination of knowledge and intuition
- Understanding how to use and apply knowledge
- Taking time to care
- Having a gentle touch
- Trusting your hands, believing what your hands are feeling and knowing what is underneath them
- Knowing when to do something and when to refer on
- Always remembering that you are the go-between from where the patient is to getting them back to better health
- A sense of humour
- Having an inbuilt sense of empathy
- To be completely present in the moment with the person we are privileged to put our hands on
- Giving a patient confidence that their symptoms will improve

Come back to this list at regular intervals, as it will remind you of all the amazing skills you have and the awesome osteopath that you are becoming/have become!

WHERE DO I START?

Planning your career

Make no mistake – being an osteopath is hard work. To build a successful practice and a long career takes dedication, determination and resilience. It's not enough just to think – 'if I build it, they will come'. You are entering a world where there is plenty of competition, where your prospective patient has a lot of choice as to where people spend their hard-earned cash, and they need to know that they will be getting value for money. One major factor which we are all still struggling with is how to get across to people what we actually do, and how we can help.

This is where your planning and decision making comes in, as you need to know from the start where you want your practice to go, stay focused on your end goal, making adaptations along the way if necessary, but always have in your mind what you want your life as an osteopath to look like. As the saying goes, failing to plan is planning to fail. So, you absolutely must have a business/life plan.

Now this is probably a statement that, like me, you have heard said or seen written many times and you thought 'well yes of course, I need to make a plan' but then never actually get round to writing one.

So, I would like you to think of the importance of writing a business plan like this.

You and I go on a cruise together. Cruises are expensive so we have saved up really hard to go on it and have an amazing adventure. As we are leaving port the captain comes over the tannoy and welcomes us all aboard saying 'Good afternoon to you all. I hope you are looking forward to a lovely cruise. I am just going to set the ship to go forward, I don't have any idea where we are going or where we will end up but that's ok for you all isn't it?'

Now how would you feel if that happened to you? You had invested a lot of time and money into the holiday, but you had no idea where you were going to go. You might have ended up somewhere you didn't want to go, or somewhere you had already been.

Think about this lack of planning and direction in terms of starting a business. You have invested a lot of money in your osteopathic degree, time and energy in developing yourself as an osteopath, and possibly even spent money on new premises. Can you see that not having a plan really isn't the best way to try to grow a successful business!

A business plan can be one page or twenty pages, and there is a lot of work to do before you even start to write it, thinking about what you want out of life, where you might live, how much you plan to save etc. However, it is best to keep it relatively uncomplicated otherwise you may find you never want to look at it again!

So please, I implore you, do this next exercise before you go any further. Print off or photocopy the blank sheet, fill it in carefully and put it in a really prominent place at work or at home where you will look at it frequently. If you see it frequently you are more likely to keep to it, be able to adapt and change it, but most importantly stick to it!

If you are struggling to know where to start a great way to begin is to SWOT!

This stands for

- S trengths
- W eaknesses
- O pportunities
- T hreats

Take a few minutes to think about each of these categories, be as honest as you can, and write as much as you feel you need to. The first two categories are fairly self-explanatory. Opportunities means things you can capitalise on, doors that you could open etc. Threats means what competitors do you have, what external forces may be relevant to your future, etc. Go to www.thetherapyrooms.co.uk. > > Survive & Thrive menu > > Enter password S&T2021#New and download the template or complete below.

Strengths	Weaknesses
Opportunities	Threats

When you have done this, if you are one of my 'Survive and Thrive' members then send it to me, and we can go through it together to make sure it is as good as it can be!

WRITING A BUSINESS PLAN

When you have completed the SWOT analysis, you will find it much easier to start to think about your business plan. Now you may well have qualifications in other subjects, or you have already worked in business so you will have a really good idea of how to write a business plan.

If not, don't sweat it, just follow the plan below, thinking carefully as you go through the questions of your answers as honestly and fully as you can.

Start with WHY you want it, then WHAT, then the HOW will follow.

My business plan dated

Why I want to be an osteopath

What are the important goals I want to achieve in my osteopathic career?

What I want my life to look like

What I want my business life to look like

What my money goals are

What my drivers are for being an osteopath (money, success, owning own practice etc)

Who are you doing this for, yourself, to please family, spouse, friends, your community

My milestones – how I will know when I have achieved my goals (new car, house, foreign holidays etc

My 5 top goals for one year are:
(Remember these need to be SMART)

S pecific

M easureable

A chievable

R ealistic

T imed

1.

2

3.

4.

5.

My top 5 goals for 5 years are:

1.

2.

3.

4.

5.

My top 5 goals for 10 years are:

1.

2.

3.

4.

5.

What I need to do NOW to start achieving my goals for year one

What I need to stop doing to achieve my goals for year one

What is my ultimate dream – my big fat hairy audacious goal (s)

As you work your way through this book, and through your career, come back to this section, read through your thoughts on why you became an osteopath. It will help to keep you on the right track and remind you of that important answer of why.

Remember – you are a business!

This is possibly one of the most important points of this book that I would really like to get you to understand and take on board right from the start.

For many years osteopaths have been expertly trained in how to be an osteopath but received little or no business training. In researching this book I contacted all the colleges and universities offering osteopathic qualifications and only one had anything near resembling any sort of business course, which frankly is shocking in 2021.

I have often thought that the reason why so many osteopaths don't have full patient lists is that they are not thinking like a business, they are not running their practices like a business, **because they don't know how to.** Look at any busy, successful practice with many associates and you will see a principal who is thinking like a business, as well as being an osteopath. The two are most definitely not mutually exclusive!

So why are osteopaths often not good business people? Lack of business training aside, it has often been thought of as a bit crude to focus on money rather than getting people better. We find the idea of someone paying for 'us', for 'our services' a bit hard to stomach, so we don't charge what we should, as we don't want to be seen as money grabbing or trying to take money off people.

Frequently osteopaths charge low fees for treatment and fail to raise fees out of fear how their patients will react. They think they won't come back, or that the patient will view them as money grabbing. In my experience, when you raise your fees you might get one or two complaining but the majority will either not notice or expect you to routinely raise your fees. If you provide them with a service, they feel is worth it then they will happily pay for you to make them feel better!

With my experience as a Master Practitioner in Neuro Linguistic Programming I know that often these thoughts and opinions come from deep rooted, subconscious beliefs, such as 'I am not worthy', 'I'm not good enough', 'I don't deserve to be paid a lot of money for my expertise.' If any of these resonate with you, then we need to have a chat about how we can stop you thinking this way and open yourself to accepting being valued for your real worth.

How to think more like a business

- Take the view that what you do significantly benefits your community. Your skills and expertise will help people to feel better, be in less pain and therefore live happier and more fulfilling lives.

- Ask yourself – are there people living in your community who need your help? Of course there are so in fact, you would be doing your local community a disservice by *not* treating them!
- The ability that you now have at your fingertips to assess, diagnose and treat your patients is an amazing skill and you should do all you can to get the message out that you really can help people to feel better again.
- Telling people about your skill set, how much CPD you do and what you can help them with often sits better with osteopaths than simply thinking about ways to get people through the door.
- Your expertise makes your local community better, and the by-product for you is that you get paid – Win Win!
- Many people nowadays are self-employed or are labourers, plasters, carpenters, plumbers etc. The longer they can't work because of their pain the more money they lose. Your skills and expertise can have them back at work sooner than if they waited for a GP visit – now isn't that a service worth paying for?
- Look at where you can add value in your local community and make sure you promote yourself rather than just thinking by advertising you are 'money grabbing'.

👁👁 I have a patient who is a self-employed plasterer. He comes in for regular treatment as he finds it helps keep his back feeling less painful when he is working. He always says if I didn't do my job then he couldn't do his job. Like I say, win-win!

And if you still need persuading here is one final way to look at the money side of the business and why you should charge your worth.

Pretty much anyone can work in McDonalds, it's not a skilled job, you can learn how to do it very quickly and therefore the wages are low.

Osteopathy – not everyone is clever enough or has the drive and ambition to undertake the years of training, study, exams, financial hardship and all-round dedication to become a highly skilled therapist. Therefore, the people who are lucky enough to come to us for treatment should pay a good amount of money to access such a skilled and highly trained individual.

Get yourself a business coach!

One of the best things I ever did to help my practice was to get a business coach. There are many business coaches out there, so it is important that you find the right one. You will know pretty quickly if they are 'your sort of person' or not. I felt it was a bit like buying a house – you know straight away if they are the right fit for you!

Why is a business coach so useful?

For many years, in fact for about three quarters of my career, I bumbled through, doing OK, but never feeling I was really reaching my potential. Then I came across a business coach whose beliefs and values resonated with me, and I decided to take a closer look at her and how she worked. I can honestly say it was the best decision I ever made.

Think about it – do you know of any world class sports teams or successful individual sports players who don't have a coach? I certainly can't, so why do we not see it as vital for our businesses to have someone by our side to help and guide us?

What are the benefits of having a coach?

- Coaches look at you and your business in a different way than the way you do. They can see opportunities and possibilities which you may never have considered or even knew about.
- They are there to encourage you, guide you, kick you up the backside if you are procrastinating too much but most of all they are there to be a support and mentor to help you to be the best and most successful osteopath you can.
- They may suggest ways of working that you had never thought of ways to help you grow your

patient list and help you to keep the patients you already have.

- They provide you with practical support as well as emotional support, which is very useful for those of us who often work on our own.

I know what you're thinking, 'Sounds like a good idea Liz, but I just can't afford one'. I understand that sentiment, I have been there myself and gasped at the cost. However, my belief is:

'If you think you can't afford a business coach, you can't afford not to have one!'

Without my business coach I really wouldn't be where I am today. I wouldn't have taken my practice to the next level, I wouldn't have added more technology to my practice, which by the way my patients love, I wouldn't have become a NLP Master Practitioner, and I wouldn't have written this book.

Have a really serious think about getting yourself a business coach, even at the start of your career. Having one will help you avoid many of the typical mistakes that osteopaths make and will get you on the right track right from the start.

Here is the link to my support site for osteopaths, and from there you will find link to my own business coach, Gilly Woodhouse at Osteobiz.

www.osteobiz.com

My advice would be to do as I did and start slowly, maybe just do a social media course with them, get a feel for how they work and if you feel comfortable with them. Then if you feel ready, have a chat with them about what they might have on offer for you to help you.

If you are worried about cost, most coaches will allow you to pay over a period of weeks and months, so you don't have to stump up the whole yearly fee all in one go. The difference that having a coach will make to your practice life will be remarkable, and you will recoup what you spend on them quicker than you realise.

THE REALITIES OF LIFE AS AN OSTEOPATH

Let's start getting down to the nitty gritty of your career and life as an osteopath, and start by asking yourself -

'What sort of career do I want?'

- *Do you want to be employed as an associate?*
- *Do you want to be self-employed as an associate?*
- *Do you want to be half working as an associate and half running your own business?*
- *Do you want to entirely be working for yourself and running your own business?*

Hopefully the answers to these questions will be clearer now you have completed your business plan.

One the great benefits of being a self-employed osteopath is that for many of us we can be our own boss; we set our own hours, fees, holiday allowances and daily lists.

However not everyone starts their career by setting up their own practice, and in fact there are many advantages to working alongside other practitioners when you have just qualified.

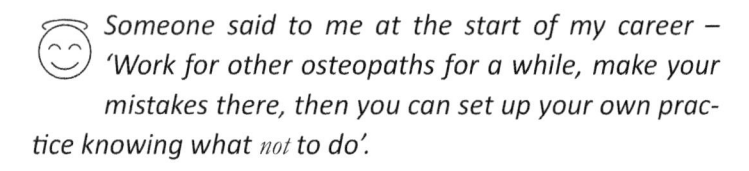

> 😊 *Someone said to me at the start of my career – 'Work for other osteopaths for a while, make your mistakes there, then you can set up your own practice knowing what not to do'.*

I spent five to six years working within two to three osteopathic practices before setting up on my own. I loved the security of knowing that I would have money coming in at the end of the week and I was fortunate to work for some fabulous osteopaths who were always there to help and guide me in those early years. I learnt a lot from them and I will always be grateful for the help and guidance they gave me. Never underestimate the value of working for someone who is experienced and who can coach and mentor you at the beginning of your career. If you are keen and willing to work you will get a lot back.

Working as an associate

Some of the benefits of working as an associate initially include:

- Getting help, guidance and mentoring from more experienced practitioners
- Spending time observing how others work and picking up hints and tips from them

- Seeing what you like, or don't like, about how others run their practices. If you decide that you want to set up your own practice, then you will have a vision or a collection of ideas that you might like to implement. You will also know what you definitely don't want to do.
- You will hopefully be busy quite quickly, which will help you build up your confidence in the early months and years.
- By working in different locations you get experienced in treating different types of demographics (more on this later).

Employed or Self-Employed?

For many years, most osteopaths who have been working as associates have been considered self-employed. This has meant that you are asked to work for a certain number of days per week at a practice, but you are not entitled to holiday pay, sick pay or any sort of pension.

This gives osteopaths a lot of freedom, as many can only come in when they have patients and are free to potentially work at a number of practices to ensure good cash flow.

However, in 2018 there was the case of The Pimlico Plumbers, which changed the stakes for the employer/employee situation.

This case centred on a plumber, Gary Smith, who worked as a plumber for Pimlico Plumbers (PP) on a self-employed basis for about 6 years. He wanted PP to see him as employed, and took them to court, winning his case. Because of how he was asked to work by PP he believed that he was a worker with limited employment rights such as sick pay, holiday pay etc. The case was won on the fact that PP exercised tight control over how he worked, his hours of work, what he wore, how much he was paid, and restrictions were placed on his ability to work for other contractors. All these conditions supported the fact that he was 'employed' by PP rather than a self-employed contractor.

As a result of this ruling and subsequent other cases in similar situations, there have been murmurings in the osteopathic community that we will have to rethink the way associate are treated. It is becoming more likely that associates will need to be treated as employees rather than self-employed, which would mean a fair salary, more rights, holiday and sick pay etc. This change is in the early stages currently, but this is a subject that the profession will need to address in the very near future.

In a more recent development, the UK's Supreme Court ruled in February 2021 that Uber drivers must be treated as workers rather than self-employed. This could mean that Uber drivers are entitled to minimum wage and holiday pay.

What type of practice do you want to work in or set up yourself?

If you haven't already done so I would strongly recommend visiting lots of different osteopathic practices, to see how they run their practice, or to spend some time learning from more experienced practitioners. You can build up a picture of the type of practice you might like to work in, or how your own practice might look one day.

To a certain extent the style of practices in your area will be reflected in the type of area you live in. For example, if you live in a big city, you are likely to find practices within other office blocks, doctors, dentists, gyms or even bike shops. The buildings may be purpose built, with shared waiting rooms and modern facilities.

If you are in a more suburban or rural environment, there is likely to be a real variety of property types housing practices. For example, my practice is in a Victorian terrace, with high ceilings and original fireplaces. Some people may be working out of their own homes or from cabins in their gardens.

Seeing how other practitioners work will help you to think about what your ideal practice might look like, whether you like modern or traditional buildings, what your thoughts are about working from home and how you might like to style your practice.

Location, Location, Location!

In all the books on how to set up a practice you will find lots of information on how to decide where to set up your own practice. It may be very obvious to you right from the start as to where you want to do this, due to where family or friends are. However, for others it might not be so clear.

👁👁 *When I graduated from the UCO, (BSO in those days) I knew that I didn't want to stay in London. For one thing even back in 1999, it seemed that the capital was already full of osteopathic practices with seemingly one on every street corner. I thought it would be very difficult to start one in such a climate. I also couldn't see myself living there for ever, so I made the decision that I would look for work outside of London.*

I worked in the Midlands for a couple of years before gradually making my way up to Cheshire in 2002. I had the opportunity to work in two to three places for the next few years, whilst setting up my own practice. I started my family in 2005 and decided to just concentrate on my own practice, as looking after kids and commuting was just too difficult for me. However, I kept in touch with my previous practice principals, as I always valued their opinions and help as I went through my career.

Sounds obvious, but you will get different types of patients depending upon where you live. Here in Cheshire, we get an interesting mix – some office workers and professionals, stay at home mums, people involved AstraZeneca (a big employer in Cheshire) and even a few farmers! I certainly didn't have much experience of treating farmers when I was at the UCO but it's amazing how you learn to adapt to the needs of your patient, to understand their working patterns and beliefs, and how you get to talk a language they understand (more on this later).

What I have also learnt from my years in practice is that you need to share the same, or similar, values of the community in which you live if you are to have a fulfilling practice life.

This doesn't mean that you have to share the same political opinions of everyone you treat or have the same hobbies. It is more subtle and intangible than that. You need to feel that your local community are 'on the same wavelength as you'. I'll give you an example:

👁️👁️ *One of the first practices I worked as a NQO was in quite a wealthy part of the Midlands. The practice was busy and had some lovely other staff working there. However, even though I liked the people I treated, I felt a bit out of sync. It wasn't until many years later that I realised why; our values were very different. This was not a criticism of them, more a reflection of my own life goals.*

This may be something which at your stage in your career you don't quite understand, or if you have been previously employed in another field you may have already experienced this feeling of not quite being in the right place for you.

This is one of the reasons I say it can be really helpful to work at different places as you really do get a different work experience at different practices, and eventually you will find your 'tribe'.

DAY TO DAY PRACTICE LIFE

How do envisage your practice day? Do you want to work five to six days a week, including evenings and weekends, or are you keen to just work part time?

Obviously if you start out as an associate it may not be so easy to make that decision as you will probably have been employed to do certain days. However, long term you may decide that four days a week is enough for you, especially if you are juggling running a business and childcare.

Think about the practicalities of working as well, such as:

- How many patients do you feel comfortable treating in a day?
- How long do you want to see each patient for?
- Do you want a break mid-morning or mid-afternoon to catch up on notes or to get back on time if you are forever running late?
- What time is a realistic start time for you? Are you a morning person who likes to start at 7.30/8am, or do you prefer a slower start to the day but are happy to work later into the evening?

- Do you want to work weekends? You will find that many patients like to come in on a Saturday, so think about how long you wish to work for and are you going to do all day, or just the morning?
- Have you thought about working on Sunday? Not many people do but depending on your religion or just your work ethic you may be quite happy to work on a Sunday. Depending upon where you live you can be sure that if you offer a Sunday you will get patients wanting to come in!

These questions often become easier to answer the longer you are in practice, as you begin to get a feel for how long it takes you to do a really thorough case history for a new patient, how long you like to treat your returning patients for, and what your natural daily work rhythm is.

Remember to take into consideration other factors including:

- Older patients tend to take much longer to get dressed and undressed. In the winter time they are likely to have many layers to take off, including thermals, corsets and all sorts of complicated underwear.
- Some patients will want to talk, a lot. One complaint that is often aimed at GPs and other medical professionals is that the patient didn't feel 'heard' or listened to. One of the best ways for

patients to feel listened to is to give them time to talk, so try to build that into your appointment time.

- Unless you want to stay late after the clinic has closed you need to remember to leave time to write up your notes. If you are using digital notes you might find you can write as you go along. If you do this remember to keep looking at your patient and not at the screen as patients will feel they are not being listened to properly if you are just typing and not looking at them.
- Breaks – yes you should take breaks during the day – if only to have a quick drink or a quick toilet trip. Keeping hydrated is something we always talk to our patients about, and we really should practise what we preach!
- It may be useful to leave some time during the day to reflect on the patients you are seeing as well as giving yourself a bit of time to breathe. In the early years you may find you need to think a bit more about your patients and your treatment plans so making sure you are not completely full can be useful. This is an important conversation to have with your principal early on. It can be a source of frustration on both sides if one party wants one thing and the other something completely different, so try to iron out these sorts of situations early on.

What type of clothing will you wear?

Once you are in practice how do you want to present yourself to your patients?

Wearing a clinic coat

- For many osteopaths wearing the uniform of a clinic coat is helpful in maintaining that professional image.
- It helps to mark you out as the professional, a visual symbol to let the patients know that the practitioner/patient relationship they will have with you is totally professional, that you are their health care worker.
- A clinic coat is easy to wear and you don't have to think about what you are going to wear each day.
- They can be very useful if you don't want to spoil your home clothes – useful if like me you treat babies and children and can get covered in all kinds of undesirable substances!

Some people however find they don't want to create that impression, that they would rather wear their own clothes. Often practitioners frequently treating children do this to make the environment less clinical for them. You may not get the choice in the early days if your practice principal requires you to wear a specific type of coat but wear what works for you if you can.

Another great way for you to look professional is to have branded workwear. There are often local embroidery retailers within your community who will provide this service – and by them knowing what you do, it is another great way to get yourself known within your local area.

Whatever you decide to wear, make sure it is clean, freshly laundered, unstained and looks professional. And don't forget a respectable pair of shoes – patients may spend some time looking at your feet during the consultation, so make sure they are clean and professional.

Online Practice Management Systems

More and more practices nowadays are using online booking platforms and patients love them! They offer them the ability to book 24/7, at a time that is convenient for them.

Think about it – how often do you prefer to book online for your GP or hair appointment, to order a food delivery, or book a table at a restaurant? It also means patients can book in to see you in the evenings, when they may have more time to plan their own diary.

There are several options available. My particular favourite is Cliniko, as it is very user friendly, has a great support service if you need help (although they are based in Australia, so you might occasionally need to wait a little longer for them to get back to you.)

Other benefits of practice management systems include:

- Easy for patients to cancel and re-arrange appointments remotely
- Invoices and receipts completed and sent to patients easily
- Put together reports on patient numbers, money earned, number of cancellations etc
- Some have a dashboard facility where you can text patients directly
- Send reminder texts and emails
- Get patients to fill in forms remotely before their appointment.
- Online notes

Other software packages include:

- Writeupp
- Jane App
- Private Practice Software

Keep on top of your accounts and get a good accountant!

Have you ever watched Dragons Den and cringed when the hopeful entrepreneur couldn't answer the questions about their finances? If you don't know what your money situation is, how much is coming in, what your expenses are, what you will need for future planning, then you really won't know how well or not your business is doing. If you are starting off your osteopathic career when you are in your twenties or thirties get into the habit of regularly saving, start a pension and/or an ISA, just make sure that you put money away for a rainy day.

(COVID-19 – when Covid-19 hit us in March 2020, most osteopathic practices closed. This meant for some osteopaths that their income completely dried up, depending upon how they had set themselves up (self-employed, limited company etc). It became obvious that many osteopaths didn't have the sufficient funds to be able to cope with not having any income for a period of time and many got into financial difficulties. All the experts say that in order to cover yourself for times like this it makes good financial sense to have at least three months' worth of money saved up. Call it 'My saving up for a rainy day/pandemic fund'!

In order to do this, start by working out what your expenses are each month, for things like rent, mortgage, car payments, food, petrol, other loans/credit cards, and times it by three. This should give you a better idea of what you would need to have saved up and try really hard to start regularly putting money away. If it helps use this tool below to start thinking about where your money goes each month.

Income and Expense Tracker   Start balance

Account	Date	Description	Category	Money in	Money out	Balance

Should I get an accounting software package?

There are a variety of accounting software packages available, all designed to help you look after your finances and make budgeting easier. These include FreshBooks, QuickBooks, Xero, Sage, Kashoo, Zoho Books and Kashflow. Any quick google search will bring up these websites where you can compare the costs and features each one has.

You will also find that here are also some free downloadable ones which might also be worth a look, so when you first start working as an associate, and if your finances are fairly straightforward these might be sufficient for you. At this stage in your career, it doesn't really make sense to spend lots of money every month on a complicated package. However, as your career progresses and your finances become more involved think about using one of these packages as you will probably find that they will save you a lot of time.

Fees

Oh, this is a tricky one! Ask any osteopath about what they charge, and you will see them turn red and mumble something about not wanting to talk about fees and money. It is one of the subjects which for some reason osteopaths find so difficult to talk about, as if money is a dirty word. Let me try and explain why this might be.

You go to a shop and you buy something. You pay for that item and you are either happy with it or you return it for a refund.

You are buying an item, a thing, something which someone else has put a value on, and you as the consumer make an informed decision about whether you feel that item is worth the amount of money you are being asked to pay for it.

When a patient comes to see an osteopath, they are not buying a thing, they are buying your expertise, experience and your time. As a profession we seem to not believe we are worthy of charging high fees, or we believe that people wouldn't come to see us if we charge too much, therefore we under sell ourselves.

Most of us struggle to put up our prices. It is not uncommon for osteopaths to charge the same treatment fee for five or more years, despite the fact that their living costs and business costs will have increased. The thought of putting up their fees brings them out in a cold sweat having had countless sleepless nights about it.

In my opinion, as a profession we don't value ourselves enough, and over my years in practice I have tried to work out why that is. For many years osteopaths worked in the shadow of modern medicine, not recognised by the GPs and consultants. In my early years working I would occasionally get patients saying to me 'Please don't tell my doctor I have come to see you, as he doesn't believe in osteopathy and says I would be wasting my time and my money in coming for treatment'. Fortunately, today we are better recognised by the medical profession, but the legacy of our past is still difficult to shake off.

What I would say to you is:

- Be proud of your qualifications and your achievements. You have worked and studied very hard to get to where you are today, and you should be rewarded for that.
- You have achieved a professional qualification which is rigorously examined and governed by a formal governing body
- Throughout your career you will be learning and developing as an osteopath, building on your knowledge base and picking up experience as you grow. You will be doing regular CPD, which costs money, and your patients will benefit from your growing knowledge.
- What have you done with your degree certificate? Or any other certificates from courses that you have attended and received a qualification for? Are they still in the envelope they arrived in or have you proudly taken them to the framers and had it beautifully framed and put on your wall? Don't leave them to gather dust in your drawers - put them on the wall. Then every time

you look at them you should feel proud of what you have achieved, it will remind you that you are an expert in your field and that yes, you really do know what you are talking about!

Other money matters - Reduced fees

Words of wisdom - Never try and guess how much (or how little) money your patients have.

Imagine the situation, you have just finished with one patient and they come into the reception area. Your next patient is waiting to see you. The first patient starts to tell you how they are really struggling for cash, how they don't know if they will be able to carry on with any further treatments as they really are in dire straits. You feel awkward and don't really know what to say.

Because you are a nice person, and because you are being watched by another patient, you say to them that they can have a reduced fee, maybe only £20 per treatment, in the hope that they will come back, and you will be able to make them better. The patient gratefully agrees, and you charge them the reduced fee.

What happens with your next patient? Do they get the reduced fee too? They can afford to pay your full fee, but why should they if you are handing out discounts today?

Our problem is that we are generally all very nice people, who only want to help people and get them feeling better.

Before you think about giving someone discount, ask yourself why you set your fees at the level you did in the first place. This is trickier if you are working as an associate, but something worth considering when you set up for yourself. Are your fees set because every other osteopath/chiro/physio etc in your area charges the same amount, or because you carefully sat down and worked out what would be a fair and reasonable rate for your services? Whatever the logic behind your thinking, how would you feel if every patient came in asking for a discount? How would you manage to pay yourself, your outgoings, your staff if you have any, never mind saving for a holiday or a pension?

It is really hard to say no to someone when they are standing in front of you in your reception area waiting to pay. A couple of ways to get yourself out of the situation and give yourself a bit more thinking time are:

- Have a notice in the practice or on your website clearly stating that you do not have a reduced fees policy. Make sure this is obvious on all your marketing/web page information - that way you can direct any person asking to your webpage to see what your policy is.

- When asked the question say that you don't think this is quite the right time to have this discussion, or that you need to think about offering reduced fees and you will get back to them. That way you can email them and let them know your decision without the awkwardness of having to say no to their face.

What you may find is that the patients who really are financially struggling won't tell you. They just won't come back for a few weeks until their next pay date. Or they may say to you directly that they need to wait until they get paid before coming in to see you.

👁👁 *I was told once by a patient that she was really struggling for money and she asked if there was there any way I could let her have a reduced fee. I was working as an associate at the time and wanted to try and keep the principal happy and make sure my list kept busy. I told her that sure, she could have a reduced fee.*

Her next visit comes, and during treatment she starts to tell me about the climbing frame she and her husband have bought for their daughter's birthday, how it took the suppliers hours to put up and how she had to not let her daughter play in the garden at all until her birthday as it was so big it took up large part of the garden. I quickly realised that she wasn't talking about a little slide and staircase from Argos, we were talking about a huge wooden structure with swings attached, ropes, a climbing wall on one side etc. Imagine how cross I was when I took her reduced fee at the end of treatment, knowing that she was more than able to pay full fee.

So my advice would be, never try to second guess the wealth or lack of it for your patients. Once you have said a patient can have a reduced fee it is very hard to rescind that offer. Think carefully about agreeing to it, or you may find yourself being resentful to that patient every time they come back in for treatment.

Now don't get me wrong, I do give a discount to some patients, but those patients have been the ones that I know really need it, and they never asked me for it, but I know that for them continued treatment would be challenging if they had to pay full price for every time. A couple of examples of the type of patient I mean are a mum of two whose husband is losing his sight due to a genetic eye condition. She is a cleaner and has had to get her 14-year-old daughter to do an ironing job just to bring more money into the house. Another patient is a divorced 75-year-old with fibromyalgia and depression who lives in one of the most deprived areas in my county and only has her state pension as income, no savings.

Other points I have picked up over time:

- Just because someone doesn't have a job, or isn't working, doesn't mean they don't have money.
- Just because someone is retired doesn't mean they don't have money.

- 'Don't judge a book by its cover' – you may get the scruffiest person coming in to see you, doesn't mean they don't have money.
- Some people will always try to get a reduction in your fee, these people just like to get a bargain/discount, doesn't mean they don't have money.
- If you offer someone a discount, rather than they ask you for it, just based on their age, how they look, their work status etc they may be offended that you think they can't afford your services.

Remember unless you are running a charity (and even they have expenses) you are a business person. You need to be able to pay your bills each month and have some money left over to invest and put towards your interests or hobbies or something lovely like a holiday. Value yourself, have pride in what you do, and don't undervalue what a difference you can make to people's lives. If you don't charge enough to keep your business going, your existing and future patients will miss out on the expertise you would otherwise have been able to provide for them.

'Free consultations and 10-minute phone chats'

You may see other practices offering free initial consultations/assessments or free 10-minute pre-appointment chats. What are your thoughts on these? Are they offered where you work? Are they something that you might like to consider offering or would you not want to give anything away 'for free'?

Within your local area you may find that other health care professionals are offering 'Free Spinal Assessments' or 'Get your first consultation for free'. There are pros and cons for this, so have a look at my thoughts on these below:

Pros:

- Encourages patients to contact you and therefore allows you to demonstrate how helpful osteopathy might be for them.
- They have already picked up the phone to you, so they already have thought that osteopathy may be helpful for them. You can use this to encourage them to come to see you.
- Often people just need to be able to speak to you and feel they can trust you before they make an appointment. They may not be sure what osteopathy is or what it can help with. Remember we know how amazing osteopathy is, the general public doesn't!
- It is a way of showing to your community that you are there to help and look after them, and that you are willing to give up some of your precious time to speak to them.

Cons:

- It can be easy to spend a lot longer doing a free consultation than you expect. Be clear with the patient at the start that it is just an assessment,

no treatment, and that you have 'x' amount of time in which to see them.
- You may get lots of people coming in for a freebie and then not converting into patients.
- Sometimes people want some help for free. Be careful how much of your valuable time you give them. You are a highly trained professional who deserves payment for your time and expertise.

HOW TO BUILD AND SUSTAIN YOUR BUSINESS WITHOUT BURNING OUT

When doing some research for this book I asked a group of osteopaths what words of advice they would give to their younger osteopath selves and what did they wish they had been told when starting their careers. It was interesting to note that we had all had similar experiences or felt the same way, so I have chosen a few of the best ones to help and guide you.

When you run your own business you need to be resilient, patient, resourceful and positive. Working as a sole practitioner can sometimes be lonely, especially if you have had a run of difficult patients or you are feeling low in energy yourself.

It can be easy to overwork, take challenges personally, feel you have to take responsibility for the health of every patient, and absorb the negative vibes that some people bring with them. For your own physical and mental health, here is a ten-step rule to stay successful and sane:

1. **Set boundaries**: Many qualified osteopaths don't put clear boundaries in place between work and home life, and when to switch off the phone and not be at work. (more on this later in the book). You need time to recharge and unwind. Don't underestimate how important this is.

2. **Be confident in your own treatment methods**: Some patients like to compare you to other practitioners. You might hear comments such as: 'My other osteopath used to do ….' It is very likely that a certain percentage of your patients will have seen another osteopath before, or possibly a chiropractor or physio (and let's be honest some don't know the difference between them!) These patients will often delight in telling you the sort of treatment their previous osteopath used to do and how they were better in one treatment.

    My advice would be never to try and emulate/copy/do the same as the previous osteopath – for starters how can you be sure that the patient remembers the sort of treatment correctly? The patient may have had a completely different problem before, and they may have been a few years younger at the time. It is always important to have had a conversation with a patient who says this to help them understand that osteopaths differ in how they treat patients, but they will hopefully be just as effective.

3. **Know when to call it quits:** Sometimes you will get an uncomfortable feeling from a patient, you don't feel at ease being in a room with them, or they just make you uneasy. Some patients are rude, some derogatory towards you. The advice overwhelmingly is if you are getting bad vibes, don't try to win them round. Say to them that you don't feel you can help them anymore and refer them on.

👁👁 *I had been qualified about six to seven years and a new patient presented for treatment. I walked into the waiting room and introduced myself. 'Well, you're not going to do me any good', was the first thing this gentleman said to me. Slightly taken aback I replied, in as polite a way as possible 'Oh, why is that?'*

He replied,' well for a start you're a woman, and my previous osteopath was a man, and there's nothing of you, so how are you going to be able to sort my problem out!'

As you can imagine, I was slightly taken aback by this comment, but putting on my professional face, my reply was something along the lines of 'Well, osteopathy isn't just about strength and force, there are many different ways of helping people get better.'

What I should have said at this point was, 'Well if that is how you feel then maybe I'm not the right osteopath for you and I will refer you on to a colleague of mine.' What I felt at this point was a bit of 'I'll show you I might be a woman but I am a really good osteopath too!'

So, I duly treated this gentleman, took the best case history, did the best examination and treatment that I could and booked him in for the following week.

The next day I am driving to work, and I receive a phone call from him. 'I won't be coming to see you next week,' says the gentleman. 'OK,' I reply. 'Can I ask why not?'

'I'm no better,' replied the man gruffly. 'I'm no better, and if you had been a male osteopath I would have been better by now, so I'm not going to waste any more of my money on you. Goodbye.'

I learnt a valuable, if uncomfortable, lesson with this patient. I knew when I first met him that I was probably onto a losing streak with him, but I so wanted to show him that I could help him, woman or not, that size and strength weren't the only way to get someone better. I so wanted to prove that I was a good osteopath and that I could help anyone in pain. I think I knew deep down that it wasn't a good idea to treat him, but I did it anyway.

The important thing about making mistakes is that we should learn from them. I've had patients come in since him who have made me feel uncomfortable like this man did, and I have known that the right thing to do is not to treat them, but to refer them on to someone else.

4. **Find your specialism and develop it:** We all finish our training with the ability to treat all sizes, shapes, genders, ages of people. You may find quite early in your

career that there are certain types of people, or age groups, or certain conditions that you prefer to treat and that you have good success with. You may develop connections within your local community which help you to develop a special interest, and if so why not go with it and become known as the 'specialist for…'. You will learn even more about the condition, become a real expert and your local community will be grateful for your expertise.

5. **'Put your roots down':** Stick to where you live/where you are and don't move around. It takes a lot of hard work and commitment to build a business. The usual quote is that it takes five years for a business to be successful, if you keep moving around you will lose the good will that you have built up and it will mean you will have to start again from scratch.

6. **Don't take it personally:** You've done your best, worked hard to improve your patient's symptoms, made a bespoke exercise routine for them, but they have come back and said they aren't any better. Any osteopath who has been in practice for a few years will tell you that they have returning patients who say they aren't getting any better. This can be really demoralising as a NQO; you feel as if you're not doing a good enough job with them, as if in some way you are failing them. But before you start to blame yourself make sure you are clear on exactly what they mean by 'not getting better'. Questions such as:

- Are they really in as much pain as when they first saw you, or are they still in some pain but it's actually not really as bad as it was? It can be easy for patients to forget the amount of pain they were experiencing initially, so it's often useful to ask them to put a scale to their pain.
- If at their initial consultation their pain felt like 9/10 to them, ask them if their pain is still at that level in subsequent treatments. What can they now do that they were finding too painful to do before they came to see you?
- And most importantly, what have they been doing since their last visit? Religiously following your advice to be careful and not do anything strenuous, or have they just been carrying on as normal and not taking care?

It is all too easy to put the blame on ourselves when patients complain that they are not improving, but remember to take the time to ask a few more searching questions before jumping to conclusions about your ability as an osteopath. Also check out the section in this book on 'Secondary Gain' – which means what does the patient gain from not getting better and what would they lose if they did get better?

7. **Keep good notes and refer back to them:** You might have a patient who claims to have seen no improvement

in their condition. Really? Are they really **no** better than they were three weeks ago? Patients will often have improved more than they realise, or more than they are prepared to give credit for. That is why on your original case history the section on Aggravating and Relieving factors not only aids your diagnosis, but it also gives you a point of reference to help the patient to see what a difference your treatment is actually making.

Gently remind them of the fact that when they first came in they couldn't put their socks on themselves, or they were having headaches every day, and now they are getting dressed no problem and their headaches are much less frequent. The penny should drop that they are in fact better, even if not entirely pain free.

Another useful tool is to have asked the patient to rate their pain level from 1-10 at their first visit, 1 being the least amount of pain and 10 being the greatest. This isn't a scientific way of acknowledging pain, but it may allow them to realise that they are in fact considerably better than they are giving credit for.

It also helps if you have explained the likely progression of their symptoms and improvement, as they will have more realistic expectations of their outcome timescale. Take time in the first/second consultations to explain how many treatments they are likely to need, how they will progress and what they can do to help themselves.

☺ *I have had this situation happen to me many times during my career, and a few years in I started to notice a pattern. If after 3-4 sessions my patient kept saying that they weren't getting any better, and I really didn't want to give up on them, I would say 'Let's just give it one more treatment, and after that if you really are no better at all then I will refer you back to your GP/specialist/etc to see if we need to get some additional tests done, like bloods or scans. I noticed that on many occasions when the patient next came in, they were significantly better. Why? Did their unconscious mind decide they needed to get better so they didn't have to have any tests or go back to their GP? I don't know the answer, but if you are struggling with a patient like this you might want to use that little technique and see if it helps to shift the way they think about and perceive the problem.*

RED FLAG ALERT – of course if someone really isn't getting any better you always need to think about red flags and if there is something you are missing. Ask more detailed questions, get a really good understanding about the person's symptoms, and reflect upon your diagnosis and treatment plan up to this point. Always remember to be safe, and if you have worries or concerns then always refer.

8. **Pace yourself:** Despite what we may think, we osteopaths are not infallible, we get tired, we need rest and time to reflect during the working day. Remember to

book breaks in your day, to have a drink or some food. It is important that we look after ourselves so that we are in the best health to deal with our patients. Being an osteopath is physically and mentally hard work at times. I learnt a long time ago that you can't do this job if you are not feeling 100% so make sure there is some time in your day to have a break.

I remember getting this advice from one of my tutors at UCO (or the BSO as it was in my day!) She said to me to remember that you need to give your 5pm new patient on a Friday afternoon exactly the same quality treatment you provided for your 9am Monday morning patient. You can't do that if you have worked yourself to exhaustion during the week and have nothing left by Friday afternoon.

9. **Give yourself a break:** Being an osteopath is hard work, and can be physically, mentally and emotionally draining. When you feel you are starting to not care as much about your patient's wellbeing, if you're getting frustrated with your little old lady patient taking an age to get undressed and dressed again then it is definitely time for a holiday or time away from work. Take the long view – rather than just looking at the near future and whether or not you can afford to take a break in the next few days or weeks, plan for your whole year. Look at your work time as over 52 weeks, or 12 months rather than week by week. Factor into your yearly budget time away from work,

as recuperation and time away is vital in maintaining your own good health.

10. **Take care of yourself:** Remember how I said that being an osteopath was hard work? Right at the start of your career, plan how you are going to look after yourself. Some things to think about are:

   - Who or what is your support network? What does it look like? Do you have a partner, spouse, family member to talk to or support you? If you'd rather not talk to someone close to you then think about getting a mentor or a supervisor as the counselling profession do. It can be really helpful to have someone outside of the profession who you can talk to and offload to, someone who won't judge you, who will support and guide you through the difficult times.

   - What sports do you like to play? What are your hobbies? Taking time out to keep these going, not just to keep yourself physically fit but also because you need to take your mind away from work and enjoy life outside of your practice! And in a roundabout sort of way you may even be connecting with your local community who might even end up coming to see you.

   - Osteopathy can be a lonely profession if you are working on your own, you will need support outside of your job to keep you happy and sane.

- Social media – there is now lots of online support and help which you may find useful. It's obviously not the same as meeting face to face, but it can be a great way to connect with other like-minded osteopaths around the world. In our post-COVID-19 world this has become an amazing way to keep in touch with friends and family, and colleagues around the world.

ARE YOU UP TO THE JOB?

Looking after your mental and physical health

Why do osteopaths self-sabotage?

Here is a story about Mr X, osteopath for about five years. A new patient comes to see him, with quite an unusual pain pattern and symptoms which could possibly have come from a number of different anatomical structures. Mr X found it difficult to make an accurate diagnosis, but using his skill, expertise and differential diagnostic thinking, came up with a diagnosis and treatment plan which he felt at time of the first treatment was correct. Mr X treated his patient twice but on returning for a third appointment, the patient reported that he wasn't feeling any better. Mr X then decided his original diagnosis wasn't quite correct, and then decided on a new diagnosis and treatment plan. Mr X told his patient about this change of diagnosis and treatment plan, and then felt as he hadn't properly diagnosed him the first couple of times that he would treat him for free for the next three sessions.

> 💭 *Was Mr X right to do this, or did he just self-sabotage himself?*

This is an interesting dilemma, but one to which really there is only one answer in my opinion. No, he wasn't right to do this, and yes, he just self-sabotaged himself and quite possibly his reputation.

Why do I say this?

> 💭 *Ask yourself this – can you always be 100% sure that your original diagnosis is correct? Of course you can't, and neither can your GP, for example. Instead, you make your diagnosis on your best diagnostic thinking at the time. That is where your hours of training and time in clinic are so important. But does that mean you will always be right? Again, of course not, we are only human, but we do our absolute best to make the best diagnosis we can when the patient is with us.*

How does it look to the patient if you treat them for free? Would you say it would have inspired confidence in his patient that Mr X treated him for free? I would think rather the patient felt he couldn't trust the osteopath, as how could he ever be sure that any diagnosis the osteopath made would be correct? What about referrals from the patient's friends or family? Would the patient feel confident about referring people to Mr X if there was a chance he might 'get their diagnosis wrong' too?

Why do you think he did it? Was he just being caring and compassionate as he was such a nice person, or did he do it because he lacked belief in himself and the only way he could make himself feel better about 'not' getting the patient better was to not charge?

Think about what you would have done in this situation, would you have not charged him (bit tricky if you are an associate) or would you have explained to him that you are going to look at a different approach for him at his next appointment and assess him every time he comes in?

INSIGHT – People self-sabotage when they have the same thought and belief patterns going round and round in their head. It's usually 'I'm not worthy' or some version of it. Having such negative beliefs don't serve you, and you need to stop them and restart with positivity. For more on how to do this visit my website.

Family Life

At some point during your career you might start a family. You may already have children, so how are you going to manage running a business and looking after children? Now I can obviously only talk about being a mother, so apologies to all the fathers and prospective fathers out there if this next section seems a bit one-sided.

Combining running a business and running a family can be tricky, particularly if you have small children who demand a lot of your time. That said, being a parent of teenagers has its challenges too, particularly if you don't want them to spend all day of their phones or the Xbox/PS5!

Childcare for the under 12s is often more available and can be a bit easier to find, as there are often more holiday clubs and activities for that age group.

Things to think about and plan for:

- How are you going to manage school holidays? Find out what holiday clubs your kids school runs and get them booked in early.
- Swap play dates with kids' parents, get grandparents on board to take kids during holidays,

Illness – for those of you who are already parents you know how often infant and junior school aged kids get ill. It can be very challenging when you know you have a full list of patients booked in and your little one starts the day with a high temperature. Make sure you have plans in place for when situations like this happen – most patients will be understanding if you need to cancel them or rearrange their appointment, not sure how many principals will be. Talk to your principal about this scenario before it happens so you have a plan in place which will kick in when this arises.

👁👁 *I was lucky when my kids were able to entertain themselves for a few hours they would come with me to my practice. I converted an attic room for them to have as their 'den' and they would read, watch films, do homework, whatever would keep them entertained for a few hours while I saw my patients. It wasn't ideal, but as we don't have any family support nearby it was the best option.*

It also allowed them to see the importance of work, they learnt great social skills, got used to talking to strangers and being polite. Later on they helped with reception duties, cashing up, filing, making teas and coffees for patients. All great skills to put on their CVs!

Holidays – very important!

You cannot do this job without having regular breaks, as you will burn out. Yes, I know that means not getting paid for the time you are away, but as mentioned above build that into your yearly accounts and planning.

Things to consider:

- What will you do with your patients while you are away? How will you ensure continuity of care? If you are working in a practice with other osteopaths, you can choose to pass them on to someone else within the practice, but if you are working on your own think about either getting a locum or making arrangements with other practices.
- You could have a mutual arrangement with a fellow osteopath whereby you look after their patients when they are away and vice versa.

Obviously, you need to be very aware of GDPR rules and not sharing patient information without informed consent, but it is a great way of making sure your patients are looked after and you foster good relations with other local osteopaths.

HOW TO TALK TO PATIENTS IN THEIR OWN LANGUAGE

'*W*ithout language, one cannot talk to people and understand them; one cannot share their hopes and aspirations, grasp their history, appreciate their poetry, or savour their songs.' Nelson Mandela

It's not always what you say, but how you say it.

How we talk to people influences our interaction with them. That may sound obvious, but it is a really important point to consider when you think about how to talk to and communicate with your patients.

As osteopaths we are blessed with knowledge, we know all the bones of the body, all the names of nerves, ligaments, blood vessels, and anatomical structures. We can recite the mnemonics for the bones of the wrist or the cranial nerves. If you are relatively newly qualified and your brain is bursting with your newly acquired knowledge which you can't wait to share with your patients.

But how useful is that for patients? Honestly, they don't care!

The majority of patients need you to explain clearly and in a language that they understand what is happening in their body, and then what you are going to do to help them. Frustrating as this is to hear as a qualified professional, it will happen a lot to you in your career. My advice – keep your in-depth knowledge for conversations with other health care professionals who will be more interested in it.

Let's explore this further. A patient comes to you with pain in their leg, really excruciating, burning pain which is worse on sitting, they have some numbness and tingling in the leg and they are limping when walking. Now you and I will have a pretty good idea of what has happened to this person, they most likely have some type of disc injury. But how to explain that to them in language that they will understand?

Here are three ways you could explain your diagnosis to them:

Example one: 'Well Mr X, from my thorough history taking and examination of you I think you have a disc herniation, probably about the level of L5 with accompanying referred pain into your lower extremity.'

Example two: 'Well, Mr X, I can see that you are in a lot of pain and from what you have told me I can be pretty certain that you have injured your lower back and spine quite badly. The pain you are feeling in your leg is being caused by nerves in your spine becoming trapped and sending pain all the way down your leg. The nerves are most likely being trapped by a disc which has moved out of place in your back. Let's talk about what we can do to get you back to feeling better.'

Example three: 'Well Mr X, what have you been doing to yourself! You seem to have popped your disc out – let's put it back in shall we?

Now I know these are very simplistic examples, but I'm sure you get the picture. Most untrained people will have heard the term 'slipped disc' and have an idea that means it has moved out from where it should be. Now of course we know what a 'slipped disc' really is, but how to explain that to someone who doesn't know what their spine looks like? What level of detail is important for them to know?

This is where your skill of reading and understanding people will be paramount. Are they the sort of person who just wants an easy-to-understand explanation and for you to get on with the treatment or do they really want you to explain it in detail? Many patients will say to you something along the lines of 'You're the expert, just get on with treatment and get me better', while you may find that others continue to ask questions until they are satisfied with, and understand, the explanation.

What I'm really trying to get across to you with these examples is to think about how your language affects your patient's understanding of what you are saying. In the majority of cases it is usually better to use less technical, more simplistic language. I do not mean by this that your patients are stupid or not capable of understanding. They just don't have your specialist training and knowledge. You may have in front of you an exceptionally bright, learned individual who is an expert in whatever their area of speciality is, but they most probably have no idea of the internal workings of their body.

When I am talking to people about the importance of language, I give the example of my first web designer. Although he built me a great website, usually when we spoke or emailed each other I didn't understand a word of what he was talking about (SEO's? Google spider? Plug ins?) and I actually felt rather stupid because of how his use of language made me feel. I would keep having to ask him to explain in simple terms what he meant.

Imagine therefore if you are a patient in pain and you are bombarded with language and information that you don't understand. How would that make you feel?

Another point to remember is that often patients will hear what they want to hear, not what you actually say, and they will remember what they want to remember, again not what you actually tell them. A perfect example of this is when the patient from the above example comes back in for their second treatment, and asks – 'So did you put my disc back last week, as I have been feeling so much better?' They heard the word 'disc', immediately thought 'slipped disc' and that needs to be 'put back'.

One point to add here is that you will have GPs, nurses and others in the health care profession as patients. You may well have professionals who are Drs in the PhD sense, who have a speciality or knowledge in the area of anatomy or physiology. You can often talk to them on a level playing field and show off your own knowledge as much as you like!

👁️👁️ *Let me tell you about a fairly embarrassing incident which happened to me along similar lines. I was treating this lovely new patient, who was a Dr, but a PhD doctor not a GP. He was struggling with his lower back and when I came to examine him I felt that he had evidence of early osteoarthritic changes in his lumbar region. Being an intelligent man, he was asking me all sorts of questions about what I thought was going on in his back, and before I had time to think, I was talking to him about the process of how OA develops and how that affects joints and in his case in particular the spine. I thought I had given a really good explanation and was happy that I had manged to get my point across in what I considered an easy to understand way.*

As the treatment continued, I started asking him about his work and found out that he had just started a new research project – all about, you guessed it, Osteoarthritis!

It was one of those occasions where I wanted the floor to swallow me up! However, he was such a lovely man that he took it all in good humour, especially when I said he probably knew a lot more about OA than I did. He is still a patient of mine to this day, but I've stopped talking to him about his work anymore, we just talk about his hobby of photography!

Being in rapport (or how to get your patient to *really* trust you)

This is a fantastic term from Neuro Linguistic Programming (NLP), meaning a sense of connection, acceptance, and openness between people, which allows communication to happen on a far more subtle level. It is the feeling you get when you sense the person who you are talking to really likes you. Rapport is the ability to enter someone else's world, to make them feel that they are understood, and that there is a strong connection between the two of you.

For us as practitioners it is that sense you get when the patient you are talking to totally feels at ease with you and opens up to you, telling you all the gold nuggets of information you need to help them on their journey to better health, because they feel they trust you.

Not being in rapport is when you feel that you're just not getting on with the person you are talking to, you sense a reluctance to be totally honest, and you know there is information they are not telling you.

There are several ways you can get into rapport with your patient, and by achieving rapport you will find you have a much better practitioner-patient relationship.

How to get into rapport – go to the website for a checklist of these.

Next time you are with a patient, or even a friend or family member, try some of these and see what effect it has.

> **Posture**: have a look at how they are sitting or standing. Are they sitting forward in the chair or relaxing back? Are they standing on both legs or are they resting more on one leg? Are their arms folded or relaxed and open? Do they have crossed legs or ankles? Are they very demonstrative when talking and make lots of large arm and hand gestures or do they keep their hands tightly together? Whatever posture they are holding, copy it or mirror it. On a subconscious level this demonstrates to the person you are talking to that you are understanding them and that makes them feel more connected to you.
>
> **Facial Expression**: If they are very demonstrative with their facial expressions then you should be too. If they are a quick blinker you blink quickly too.
>
> **Breathing**: Match their pattern and location of breathing. Is their pattern lots of short, quick breaths or do they take long slow inhalations. Try to mirror whether they seem to be upper or lower rib breathers too.

> **Voice**: Match their tone, quality, raspiness, volume. If their speaking voice is deep, then lower your tone slightly, not in a comical way, but if your timbre is higher try just lowering it a touch. Alternatively, if your voice is deeper, then raise the tone a little. How quickly or slowly does the person speak? Listen to their speed and volume and that will help getting into rapport even more.
>
> **Words**: Now I love this one, as it means you have to listen really hard to what the other person is saying and work out the type of words they most frequently use. By that I mean are they using visual ones 'Do you see what I mean?', or 'I don't feel that is right for me (kinesthetic) (more on this below). It may take a little while for you to work out what their dominant word type is, but when you do you can reflect the language they use back at them and they will feel that you understand them.

The type of words we use

Let's go into a bit more detail about words, as this is really useful in practice. If you can talk the same language as your patient, they will feel more understood and if they feel more understood they are more likely to trust you and respect what you say. They will also feel more listened to, particularly if you can reflect their words back to them.

In NLP we use the word 'Predicates'. These are the words or types of words we use to describe our inner world to the outside world. The nervous system and the mind, through which our experiences are processed use the following five senses:

They are Visual, Auditory, Kinesthetic, Olfactory and Gustatory or VAKOG.

The way we code, order and give meaning to language and other non-verbal communication uses language in the following ways:

- Pictures
- Sounds
- Feelings
- Tastes
- Smells

The way we see the world and the words we use to describe our experiences and our behaviours are usually sensed by us most dominantly by one of the above. For example

- I see what you mean (visual)
- I hear what you're saying (auditory)
- That felt wrong for me (kinesthetic)
- I could smell the danger of the situation (olfactory)
- It just wasn't to my taste (gustatory)

When you listen to the words your patient uses you will start to understand which predicate they use. Here are some typical examples you are likely to hear in practice for you to have a go with. As you read them, work out what sense the sentence uses.

- 'I feel under a lot of pressure at work'
- 'In my mind's eye I imagine the pain as a hot poker in my back'
- 'What you are saying rings a bell with me'
- 'My leg feels solid, like a dead weight'
- 'It was a bitter blow for me when I couldn't go to work'

How is this useful in practice?

When you first take a case history from a new patient, listen carefully to not just what they are saying but also the types of words they are using to describe their pain or life experiences. Jot down somewhere on your case history form what is their dominant predicate (VAKOG), and each time they present in clinic reflect their style of words back to them. Don't worry if you struggle to do this to start with, it takes practice, but if you make this a habit you will soon find you hear the words easily. This is a great way of getting quickly into rapport with them and will make for a really productive treatment.

HOW TO DEAL WITH 'DIFFICULT' PATIENTS

'A genuine smile from a 'difficult' patient' is enough to make the entire shift feel worthwhile'.

What is a 'difficult' patient? What would your description be? Someone who asks lots of questions? Challenges your diagnosis? Someone who won't answer your questions or gives evasive answers? Someone who is a bit rude or aggressive? Someone who's not getting any symptom relief or simply someone that you don't like?

Whenever I come across a patient I would consider 'difficult' I always ask myself these questions, as understanding why someone brings out this emotion or feeling in you helps you work out the best way to handle the situation.

Even as a relatively new osteopath at the start of your career, you will have a good grip on basic body language, and you may already have experienced that situation where you walk into the waiting room and you can 'feel' the tension. You will be aware of the patient's posture – how are they sitting, standing, pacing?

Remember – you are not seeing people at their best, or as we say in NLP language 'People are not their behaviour'.

When patients come to see you, they will most likely be in pain, and that pain may be physical, emotional or spiritual. They will be hurting, uncomfortable, maybe cross or angry, frustrated that they can't do what they want to do, and looking to you for help and advice. They may also be apprehensive or nervous. Some may be anxious about undressing in front of you, while others may be concerned that you will not take their condition seriously. This may be because they have consulted other healthcare professionals previously, and not had the experience they had expected.

Hopefully in your training you will have come across similar situations which will have prepared you for the 'angry' patient, but here is some advice as to how to help you deal with this situation.

If you are lucky enough to have a receptionist this is another area where they are invaluable. Any good, experienced receptionist will have spotted this type of patient, and if they are trained well will hopefully have already tried to diffuse the situation. They may have tried chatting to them, explaining the treatment process to them, maybe even talking about their own personal experience of osteopathy. If they haven't managed to work their magic then they may well warn you before you take the patient in for treatment.

Greet them with a smile and a happy, positive demeanour. It is hard to be too angry with someone who is smiling at you!

Once in the treatment room, be aware of their body language – how is your patient sitting, remember the classic defensive/angry pose of crossed arms, crossed legs and sitting back in the chair? If your patient is sitting like this, make a mental note of this and get a strategy going in your head of how you are going to ask your questions so that you get all the relevant answers, whilst trying to encourage your patient to feel less defensive and comfortable.

It is important with patients like this that they are made fully aware of the type of questions you are going to ask. As osteopaths we ask a lot of questions, and they may not be used to this type of questioning. If they don't understand your line of questioning, then they may become more aggressive and you will have lost their trust.

I have often found that once you have these patients on-side they are really grateful for what you can do for them, you just need to show empathy, understanding and kindness.

How to deal with political/racist/sexist comments from patients

This is something which regrettably you will experience in practice life, not hopefully directed at you but there will be comments that you may find offensive. Knowing what to say or do, or what not to say or do will be vital if you are to remain professional and not end up arguing with a patient in the therapeutic environment.

In my own life as an osteopath I have worked through the bombing of the Twin Towers, Brexit, the #MeToo movement and Covid-19 to name but a few. Often the osteopath's couch is the place where people want to chat and discuss current events, but how to keep professional when your patient may have completely opposing views to you? You may be shocked by what some people say but remember not to judge them on their opinions and treat them with professionalism at all times.

Make it clear right from the start of their experience at the practice that racist/ sexist or offensive language or behaviour will not be tolerated. A clear, politely worded poster in the waiting room stating the practice policy of universal tolerance to all is one way to ensure that patients are clear on what is acceptable. However even this may not avoid all unnecessary or unpleasant comments from being voiced.

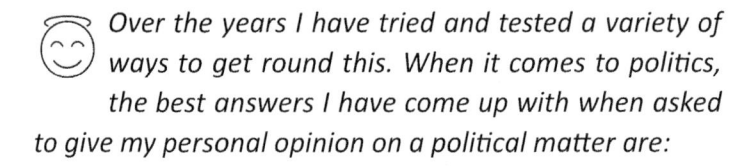

Over the years I have tried and tested a variety of ways to get round this. When it comes to politics, the best answers I have come up with when asked to give my personal opinion on a political matter are:

- 'I decided many years ago that I wouldn't discuss politics with patients, so I'm not going to say anything about ...'

- *'I prefer not to give my personal opinions on matters like that.'*
- *'I like to keep politics out of the treatment room, let's talk about something more fun!'*

Patients seem to be quite satisfied with these statements, and it gets you out of any further tricky discussions.

Racist comments

How to deal with those racist comments that shock you or make your skin crawl?

Depending upon what kind of working environment you are in (i.e. working on your own or as an associate) I would suggest dealing with it is one of the following ways:

One-off comments – if you are concerned and you are working as an associate I would strongly suggest that you talk to your principal about the comment, making them aware early on that you have concerns about the beliefs of this patient and that you find it unacceptable. You may find that the patient has voiced similar opinions previously with others in your practice, and if so it will be up to the principal to make a decision on what to say or how to continue having the person as a patient.

If the comments happen more than once during the consultation you may need to decide how you want to handle it there and then. One simple way is just to say:

'I'm sorry but I don't think that is an appropriate comment and I would be grateful for you not to continue talking in that way.'

It may create an awkward feeling in the treatment room, but it is important for the patient to know that as a practitioner you do not tolerate that sort of language/behaviour.

If you don't want to address the comment during the treatment process, then decide what you are going to say when the appointment comes to an end, and in a calm and polite manner have the conversation.

In both these cases talk to your principal, or if you are working on your own then contact a trusted colleague. It is always good to talk through your worries with someone more experienced than you and make others aware of your situation.

You should also record what was said very carefully in your notes and any reaction or comments from the patient as well.

I don't want you to worry that this kind of situation is a regular occurrence, in my experience that is not the case. I think it is just invaluable to have thought about how you might behave in a situation like this and have a plan in place which is easy to execute.

Beware of the male patient booked in by their wife/partner!

Now I really am not being sexist here, but time and again I have seen male patients booked in by their wives/partners who are sick of them complaining about their pain and not doing anything about it. You will know very quickly who these patients are as they will probably greet you with: 'My wife/partner/girlfriend booked me this appointment', accompanied by the 'angry pose' described above (arms and legs crossed, siting back in the chair etc).

The wives/partners are usually existing patients who value what we do, and who want their partners to experience the same benefits from treatment that they have had. However, some male patients have a problem with admitting that they need help, and so find it difficult to ask for help. Coming in for treatment, especially when they didn't make the decision to book in the first place, might feel to them like they are not in control of the situation and some men find that hard to deal with/don't like that.

Suggestion on how to deal with this:

- When faced with someone with this attitude, it is best not to be patronising or belittle them. Instead use language like: 'Well I'm sure they/your wife/partner only have your best interests at heart', or 'they must really care for your wellbeing if they have done that for you', rather than 'well they probably got fed up with you complaining!'

- Explain that what you will aim to do in the consultation is to really listen to their concerns, and then together decide what would be the best way to move forward from where they are. Engaging a patient like this into the whole process allows them to feel that they have control and input into a situation where they may originally have felt that they didn't have any.
- Giving patients exercises to do really helps them to gain a sense of control over their problem as well.
- Setting small goals together can be helpful in helping them see that coming in for treatment is the start of them getting better, but that they have more power/control themselves if they follow a plan set by them and you.
- Be genuine and compassionate, professional yet friendly and you will probably find your magic hands will easily win them over and they will become your biggest fan!

The Patient Who Won't Get Better

Secondary gain

This is another great NLP term which I have found invaluable in clinical practice. Secondary gain can be explained as what value does the patient have in their life currently for not wanting to get rid of their pain or problem? What about their life is 'better' for having the problem and what advantage might they lose if they were symptom free?

You may have heard of tutors in clinic or your practice principals say things like 'there are some patients who don't want to get better' and this is exactly what secondary gain is.

👁👁 *Here is an example from my own practice. Mr T comes in for treatment with elbow pain. He has been diagnosed with upper limb disorder or RSI by his GP and has already been signed off for four months. He is due to go back to work in the next couple of weeks but is still in quite a lot of pain so has been referred by his manager for some additional treatment. During the consultation Mr T tells you that he has been suffering from depression as well as the arm pain, and has not been doing much at home, being looked after by his wife and children, getting up late, watching a lot of TV etc. He is on full pay. He says that when he is at home resting his arm doesn't hurt much, but the minute he starts to do anything strenuous, even just emptying the dishwasher, he gets the pain again.*

He doesn't admit that he doesn't want to get better, but can you see where the advantage is for him to stay as he is? His life is very easy at the moment, he doesn't need to do much around the house, has an easy life and the pain isn't troubling him much when he doesn't have to work. This is a perfect example of secondary gain.

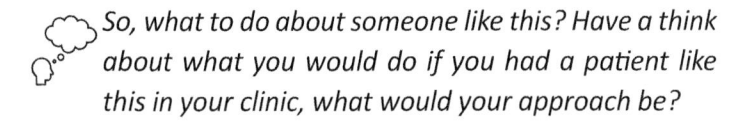

So, what to do about someone like this? Have a think about what you would do if you had a patient like this in your clinic, what would your approach be?

Here's what I would do:

- **Be honest with him** – acknowledge his symptoms and his pain and show him that I understand his situation and his desire not to make his pain worse.

- **Be enquiring** - does he really never want to go back to work? Is there something else at work which he is reluctant to return to, something in the work environment which is making him reluctant to return? For example, a difficult work colleague, or boss? Is the work not fulfilling or is he feeling out of his depth? I would suggest not immediately jumping to the conclusion that he is simply lazy by not wanting to go back, there could be many other reasons for his secondary gain attitude.

- **Be realistic** – if he really doesn't want to go back work, how effective a practitioner will I be if his subconscious mind is telling him not to get better? This may be one of those situations where I would need to be honest and realistic with myself in order to get the best outcome.
- **Phased return to work** – if I manage to get a deeper understanding of his situation, a good way to help a patient is to give them back some control. Talking through a phased return to work is a great way for them to feel they have some say in their onward recovery and gives them reassurance that they don't have to go back into exactly the same situation as they were in previously.
- **Continuing care** - reassure him that I will be there to continue to help him so that he will make a good recovery.

THE MAGIC IS IN THE RELATIONSHIP – DEVELOPING A DEEPER UNDERSTANDING OF WORKING AS AN OSTEOPATH

'Osteopaths don't treat symptoms, we treat people'.

This is a phrase that you will hear a lot of during your career. You may find it a bit simplistic, but the magic of osteopathy happens when we build a relationship with our patients and they know that they can trust us and that we will help them.

Have you ever had the experience when talking or interacting with someone that you are the most important person in the world at that moment, and that the person you are talking to is really listening to you and is super interested in what you have to say? That is the sort of relationship you should aim to have with all your patients.

So how do we do this?

We do this by listening, understanding their concerns and acknowledging their symptoms, something which they may not have experienced from other health care professionals. Patients may say things like – 'This is going to sound a bit strange but...' and then tell you about some strange condition that they have. Always try to be empathetic when someone is telling you their problem, as for them the problem is real. They may be trying to articulate something as best they can but with difficulty. They will only do this if they believe they can trust you and that you understand them.

Being listened to is one of the most valuable experiences in a therapeutic relationship. Most of us in private practice are in an enviable position to be able to spend time with our patients, a luxury that certainly GPs don't have. Never take that time for granted, give your patient time to talk and make sure you really listen to them. You need to be present, interested and compassionate at all times. If you don't feel you can be, then it is time to have a break from your clinic and get some well-deserved rest and recuperation.

Knowing how to build a relationship with patients takes experience. You will have had experience of this when you were at Uni, and the longer you are in practice the easier it will become. You will start to see similarities in patient behaviour, the type of language they use and what questions you need to ask to find those gold nuggets of information which will help you with your diagnosis and treatment plan.

Take time regularly throughout your career, but particularly in the first few years, to reflect on your work. Look at the patients who have a really good response to treatment, and those that don't have such a good outcome. Reflect on what the differences are, was it simply that the patient's symptoms were not as severe, or was there something in the therapeutic relationship which could have been better? Getting into the habit of regularly assessing yourself and how you are doing is a great way to develop yourself as a practitioner, and it helps with your CPD as well.

CREATING A HEALTHY RELATIONSHIP BETWEEN PRINCIPAL AND ASSOCIATE

The relationship between associates and principals can either be fantastic and productive, or difficult and challenging. How each person in the relationship plays their part will determine the fate of the relationship, and it is up to each to do their best to make it the most productive it can be.

Let's consider some of the factors that go into a healthy principal/associate relationship and let's start by looking at it from the associate's position.

Looking for an associate position:

When you are looking for a position as a new associate, what factors about where you are going to work are important for you? Start by brainstorming all your ideas and then rank them in order of importance for yourself. You might come up with something this looks like this:

- location of work
- distance from friends/family

- rural or city
- ease of transport links
- hours of work and rate of pay
- size of team
- lone work/teamwork days required
- what support is on offer
- specialism required

So, having some idea of what you are looking for will help you make the first step in deciding what type of practice you are looking for, or what sort of work would suit you.

The Interview:

Once you have been through this process and you have secured an interview, the next thing is to prepare yourself for it.

One important thing to do before any interview is to consider what type of questions you might get asked and how you would answer them. Ask your friends and colleagues if they have already had an interview what they were asked.

Questions you might get asked:

- What made you choose to be an osteopath (obvious one but need to be prepared for it!)

- Why do you want to come and work at this practice?
- What can you bring to the practice?
- Give me an example of a difficult patient you have seen, why it was difficult and how did you manage the situation?
- Do you have an idea of any training or areas of expertise you might like to develop?
- How long does it take you to get to here from your home?
- Are you looking to just work here, work here and elsewhere, or work here and also work for yourself?

How to smash the interview!

Some of the suggestions below might seem very simplistic for those of you having osteopathy as a second career but having been an associate and a practice principal myself, and speaking to other principals, these points really matter when you go for an interview.

1. Dress smartly. Casual clothes or jeans just will not do! You are a professional and you need to show that you are. Making a good first impression is very important.
2. Make sure you know where you are going and work out how long it is going to take you to get there by car, public transport etc. If you are

driving find out where the nearest parking is so you're not desperately trying to find somewhere.

3. Give yourself plenty of time to get to the interview, it is always worth arriving early rather than panicking and being on the last minute. One thing which won't impress your prospective boss is if you turn up late.

4. Be friendly and polite to the reception staff. I always ask my receptionists what they thought of the person who has come for interview – they will be working with them too so it is important to get their view on the individual too.

5. Smile! It's not always easy to smile when you are nervous, but your prospective boss will want to know what your interpersonal skills are and a happy demeanour will seriously help you.

6. Turn up for your interview – this may seem like a crazy thing to write, but the number of times I have heard that associates simply haven't turned up for their interview amazes me!

7. Make sure you have booked time out of where you are currently working in good time so you don't upset your existing boss or patients by having to rearrange everyone.

8. Have a list of questions which you want answering and make sure you get them answered. In particular, questions about pay rates and/or percentages, holidays, what hours you will be required to work,

what is their policy on retainers or sick pay. Make sure you know what support you will have from the principal. Will they be working with you at the same time, or will you be on your own with or without a receptionist? What kind of patient booking system do they use and what training will you receive on how to use it? Would you be self-employed or employed? How long before the first patient does the principal like the associates to arrive? These can be difficult questions for some NQOs to ask but they need to be sorted out right from the start.

9. Get a sense of what type of practice the principal is running and what they want from you. By this I mean are they forward looking, keen to expand, good with social media, wanting to help and support you, or are they simply looking for you to be a 'cash cow' and not offer any guidance or help for you at all? If that's what you're looking for then great, but I know a lot of NQO's need and want some support in the early years.

10. In the same way, be honest and clear with the principal what it is that you are looking for. Most NQOs will want help and support – I can remember even asking my principal to do an HVT for me on a patient I was struggling with! So be upfront with your prospective boss about what is right for you.

You've got the job!

Hurrah! You were successful in the interview and you are now working as an associate in your new post.

Unless you are talking over from an existing osteopath it is likely that your list might look a bit thin for a few weeks. Don't panic, this is quite usual, but think about what you can do to help build your list.

Things to help list build:

- **Testimonials**: Get used to asking all your patients for testimonials and referrals. Getting into the habit of doing this early in your career is a great way to build up your confidence and your list. Something along the lines of 'You know I love helping people get out of pain and back to better health. If you know someone who is struggling like you were before you came to see me then please send them my way as I'd love to see if I can help them too.' There is no mention of money in this way of saying things, so you needn't feel awkward. And when you help the person your patient referred, your patient will be so happy that they managed to help someone too!
- **Social Media**: Use social media regularly. Of course, check with your principal before embarking on a campaign, but it is likely they will be more than happy for you to take the lead in this. If you

are unsure how to do this then Gilly Woodhouse runs a great social media course (www.osteobiz.com) and will show you what posts work and what doesn't work, how not to spend huge amounts of money on marketing, and how to really get the message across of what we do as osteopaths.

- **Facebook Lives**: Do lives – yes I know that sounds scary, but if you just think that you are only talking to one person that really helps. Lives help to raise your profile on Facebook and people love them. Don't worry if you don't look amazing, people are much more interested in what you have to say and the advice you can give them rather than what you look like. Again, Gilly can really help you here with how to do these.

- **'See how you go'** – these words should NEVER EVER be said to your patients. This is one of the biggest mistakes that NQOs make when they first qualify. They often feel awkward about asking patients to come back as they haven't quite got over the 'charging people for treatment' problem. However, if you finish a treatment by saying that patients often feel unsupported, uncared for and may well seek help elsewhere rather than following up with you. I feel it diminishes your standing with them as the professional in the relationship. And what does 'see how you go' actually mean? How is the patient supposed to know if their symptoms warrant more treatment or if they should just wait until they start to ease? You will build a lot of respect and confidence in your work as an osteopath if you properly look after patients and provide them with a proper treatment plan.

- **Always have a treatment plan**: explain your treatment plan to your patients and why you feel a follow up is important. That way your future list starts to look busier, and if patients then decide not to keep that appointment it's their choice rather than you not looking after them properly. Also, you help the patient by explaining what is involved in the treatment plan, and how they can play their part. As I mentioned above, giving patients more control over their own health and wellbeing can be very empowering for them.

Early on in my career one of my close friends went to see an osteopath for some treatment as they had been recommended to him. When we had a chat later about how his treatment was going, my friend said to me that the osteo had suggested a couple of treatments over the coming weeks until they felt that my friend's symptoms had improved. I thought my friend might have seen this as 'money grabbing' or might have felt that the osteo was taking advantage of him being in pain. Instead, my friend was delighted that the osteopath had offered this type of care package, he said to me that he felt looked after and was quite happy to follow the osteopath's advice as, to use his words 'He's the expert and knows what he's doing'.

Other ways to be a great associate:

1. Work hard, turn up on time for work, be enthusiastic for work and go the extra mile for your patients and the practice. Your hard work and dedication will be rewarded.

2. Greet your patients with a smile, a good morning and use their name when you greet them. If the patient is new, introduce yourself by telling them your name. Be friendly and enthusiastic when you greet them, it will make them feel more comfortable and at ease.

3. Be helpful and pro-active around the practice. If you see something which needs doing, like washing up cups, emptying bins, refilling tissue boxes, then take the initiative and do it. You will win brownie points not just from the boss but from your practice manager too.

4. Be honest and truthful – and don't steal from the practice. Again, this may sound like a crazy thing to say but it has happened to colleagues of mine. I don't mean accidentally putting a biro in your bag at the end of the day, but stealing paper, medical supplies or equipment.

   I think the worst example I heard was of an associate was a bit short of money before the end of the month when he was to receive his payments. He decided to forge the signature of his boss on a cheque he wrote to himself. Really not a good idea, and the principal was less than impressed when he found out.

5. If you are unhappy about something, or unsure of something then speak up. It is always best not to let things fester or to allow little things to escalate into bigger problems.

6. Be honest. If you have done something wrong, or made a mistake, put on your big pants and own up to it. Lying to your boss, like stealing, is never a good idea. It is not easy always easy to admit you have made a mistake, but the consequences of not owning up are often much worse. The sooner you explain what has happened, the quicker your boss can help you put it right, and they will respect you more.

7. Be prepared to muck in and help out with other things at the practice. Doing other jobs around the practice also helps you appreciate how an osteopathic business works, whether it is changing towels, refilling the paper towels in the bathrooms, taking payments or booking people in for their next appointment. These are all really useful ways of learning how to run a business and will give you an idea of how you would do things if you decided to set up your own one day.

> *I used to work at a lovely practice where there was always reception cover and if one of the receptionists was poorly the practice manager always managed to get someone to cover. One afternoon the entire reception team was struck down with a terrible cold, leaving myself and my boss having to look after the practice ourselves. I had a spare appointment slot so I phoned all the patients for the next day to remind them of their appointments. My boss was very grateful that I had, as it meant she didn't have to do it at the end of her long day. Brownie points for me!*

Moving onwards and upwards: How to be a great principal

So now let's look at it from the point of view of being a great principal. I know this may seem slightly out of the remit of this book, as it is mostly intended for NQOs. However I felt it was important to get perspective from both sides of the associate/principal relationship. I also hope that when, or if, you decide to become a principal yourself you will have a better understanding of how to be not just a great principal, but how to bring out the best in the people that work for you so that they will stay with you for a long time and really enjoy working for you.

Taking on an associate:

Start by thinking about what you are looking for in an associate. You may want to consider things such as:

- How experienced are they? Are you looking for someone fresh out of Uni, or someone with a bit more experience?
- If you are happy to take on an NQO, what sort of person are you looking for? Are you looking for a team player or someone who prefers to work on their own? How much support are you willing to give them, as many will need and want some help and support in their first couple of years out of Uni.
- Career path – how do you envisage your NQO developing at your practice? What kind of career path can you offer them, and how can you help them to become the best osteopath they can be? If this isn't something you want to do, then I would think very carefully about why you want to take on an associate.
- Involve your associates in matters to do with the practice. No one will ever be as passionate or enthusiastic about your business as you are. However, if you aim to get your team more involved in the business then you are likely to find that they want the practice to flourish and do well

as it reflects on them too. How to do this might include simple things like:
- getting them involved in some of the decision making at the practice, even it is only things like what sort of coffee and biscuits to have, what type of couch roll do they prefer etc.
- having social nights out to learn a bit more about them out of the work context.
- having regular practice meetings where matters to do with the running of the business can be discussed.
- asking them to contribute to the social media posts you put out, get them to write some blogs or do Facebook Lives, anything in the social media world where they feel they can make a difference.
- See if they have a particular speciality or interest that they would like to work more with, for example sports people, the elderly or acute injuries.

- Whatever you can do to help your employees feel more like they are part of a team and not just workers will help to keep them happy and motivated.
- Pay them a decent salary. There is much discussion in our profession at the moment as to upcoming changes around how associate are paid. At the

current time of writing some associate are paid on a per patient percentage, some have a retainer and that is topped up if they see more patients. Very few are salaried, but it may be in the future that this is the way forward.

- Unfortunately, there is a high dropout rate for osteopaths in the first few years after qualification. It is not entirely clear at the moment why this is happening, but one suggestion is that for most NQOs the salary they get just isn't sufficient for them, or they feel for the amount of work they do the remuneration is not good enough.
- Treat your associate with respect and compassion. Try to remember how you felt when you first qualified, the feeling of sometimes being overwhelmed if you had to see several new patients in one day, the worry that you have done 'something wrong' with a patient and how to sort it out.
- If something is bugging you, get it sorted quickly, don't let it fester and become a big issue. Remember for some NQO's this is their first real job, so be prepared to cut them a bit of slack if they are not quite up to scratch as quickly as you would like them to be.

DIFFERENT VALUES/ DO YOU SEE EYE TO EYE?

One useful point that I learnt from my training as an NLP practitioner is that people have different values when it comes to all aspects of life, and work is no different. Some people love stability and will stay doing the same job for years, solidly working for the same or similar reward and not complaining. Others will change their job every 7-8 years as they look for a new challenge. Some will always be looking for new ways to stimulate themselves, changing jobs or job roles very frequently as they like to have new challenges.

This type of information is very useful to know and can help employers understand the needs of their employees better. For example, if one of your employees is happy and willing to stay in their job for many years, then they may require very little input from you. They are happy with the status quo, don't like things to change, and have the work value of 'work hard now and I will get the reward when I retire'.

However, if your employee likes variety, then in order to keep them you might need to change a few things about their work environment. For example, they may regularly need to change where they sit or how their room is laid out. They may need challenges to keep them interested in work, whether that is giving them tasks to do within the running of the business or asking them to come up with new ideas of how to do things.

The more challenging person to have on your team is someone who gets bored easily and needs to keep doing new things or moving around. This may be you, in which case if you are working as an associate it might be important to make your principal aware of this so that you can incorporate ways to counterbalance this within your place of work without constantly moving practices.

Being aware of different people's values and how they like to function at work will be vital to a healthy and constructive working relationship.

Looking after your own Mental Health

Boundaries

What is a boundary and why they are so important?

Boundaries are 'the decisions we make which govern our behaviour and the way we interact with others. A sort of personal code which may change with time and circumstance.' ('Boundaries: How to draw the line in your Head, Heart and Home' Jennie Miller and Victoria Lambert)

Do you think you have any boundaries in place? If you are asked to do something, and you really don't want to do it, you don't have time for it, or it is something that you have done hundreds of times in the past and you are fed up with taking the responsibility for it, what do you do? Do you still say yes you'll do it, or do you politely but firmly say no?

If you struggle to say no to people, whether that is friends, family or work colleagues, now might be a really good time to take a look at that and work out why. Often being unable to say no is because you haven't put any boundaries in place and so people can't respect them as they are not there to respect.

Take a look at these two scenarios:

Scenario 1

Mr B is a recent graduate and has been working in his new role as an associate for 2 months. His principal is happy for him to work extra hours in addition to his contracted hours, even Saturdays or weekends, if Mr B is willing to do so.

Mr B is contacted by a new patient who says she would like to book in for an appointment but she can only come after work, and around 8pm would suit her best. Mr B usually finishes around 6.30 to 7pm as he has a 40-minute drive home after clinic, but on this occasion, as the lady is new to the practice, he decides to make an exception.

The new patient turns up, the consultation goes well, and Mr B says he would like to see her again next week, and he offers her 7.30pm, in an attempt to finish a bit earlier. The patient reluctantly agrees, but a couple of days before her appointment phones up to ask for her appointment to be moved to 8.30pm as she can't make it any earlier. Mr B, wanting to please the patient as well as keeping the principal happy reluctantly changes the appointment to the later slot, but feels rather frustrated that he is doing this as he will have to change his own plans for that night.

The patient continues to have treatment for the next few weeks, always late in the evening and Mr B always agrees to it. He thinks being a NQO he just needs to put up with the late nights, even though he doesn't like finishing so late. He also finds that other patients start to be booked in late at night without him being asked. He becomes resentful at this and doesn't look forward to his late nights at the clinic.

Question: how do you feel about this scenario? Do you think Mr B is right to work around the needs of the patient and as a NQO yourself would you do this too? Or would you insist that the patient comes at a time to suit you and explain this to your principal and the reception staff?

Scenario 2

Ms C is a relatively new osteopath and mother to a young baby. She has just come back to work after her maternity leave and is having to juggle childcare and running her own practice. As a result, she is squeezing her patients into the late afternoon and evenings when her partner is at home and can take over parental duties.

She is finding that several of her patients are becoming quite difficult when it comes to booking appointments. Due to her reduced hours Ms C is not offering as much choice of appointment times and as she is such a great osteopath her evening slots are getting booked up quite quickly.

Several of her patients are becoming quite picky with their times and are wanting to get the same time every week, getting annoyed with Ms C when they can't do this. Some are even asking her to call up the patients who are already booked in and get them to move their appointment times. Ms C feels anxious and worried about what to do, as she wants to keep her patients happy but feels pulled between her role as mum and her role as an osteopath.

Question: What do you think Ms C should do? Should she phone the other patients and ask them to move? Should she work longer into the evening to fit everyone in and earn more money? Or should she stick to her guns and just do the hours she has set aside to work?

Both of these scenarios are ones that you will face frequently when you are in practice. No matter how many hours you make available for patients, there will always be those that try to take advantage of your kind nature and want to come in at different times.

Patients will do this if you haven't set your boundaries clearly enough.

Start your career by being strong and setting your boundaries early on in your career. Of course, you can change them as you wish. Think about how you want to work, what hours you are prepared to make yourself available and realise, as I've said many times in this book, you are a business, this is your business and you set the rules, not your patients. Set your hours and stick to them. Of course, you can always add the occasional patient in at a different time if you feel you want to, but this should be done on your terms, not because you feel pressurised into doing it by a patient.

Here are a few ways that you might find useful to help you do this.

- Be very clear in all your communications with your patients, whether that is on your website, newsletters you send out, social media etc, what your hours are. It is often not a good idea to put on your website that you are open 7am-7pm just so it looks good but never really to have the intention of being at work at 7am.
- Don't give the patient much choice of appointment times. Say 'I have 4.30 Wednesday or 5pm

Thursday available, which would you like?' That way they have to make a choice of only 2 slots, rather than asking them when they would like to come in. (Note – if/when you have your own receptionist make sure you train them to understand this as well).

- If they really can't do those times you offer, then say 'I can just see that someone has cancelled at 5.30pm on Thursday – that's lucky isn't it! Shall I book that one for you?' Then the patient goes away feeling lucky that they have managed to secure a spot and you are happy that you have stuck to your guns and haven't been made to compromise.

- Patients are often more flexible than they may seem. Over the years I have been in practice I have found the more choice of times you give patients, the more choice they will want. Be strong, stick to your hours, and you will be surprised how flexible patients will be.

- And finally, I would urge you not to see this as being unkind to patients or that you are not a nice person for not offering 24-7 appointments. Working to the hours that you want to work is the best way to ensure you look after your own personal, physical and mental health. Don't be worried that the patients will go elsewhere if they can't get the time that suits them, yes you might lose the odd one, but it is unlikely to have a significant impact on your overall patient list.

If you are struggling with the concept of boundaries, or you would like to learn more about how to set them, then I would highly recommend the book 'Boundaries: How to draw the line in your Head, Heart and Home' by Jennie Miller and Victoria Lambert (published by Harper Collins). It is a great introduction to the concept of boundaries, with lots of really helpful exercises to do to guide you into understanding what your own boundaries are and how to set them.

THE BORING BUT NECESSARY BITS

*P*olicies and Procedures.

Think you can just rent a space and start working? Think again!

When you start any business it is vitally important to know that you have all the correct policies and procedures in place BEFORE you open your doors. By having everything in place, should a tricky situation arise, you will have thought about it, written a policy document about it, and have it filed somewhere safely for you to look at when needed.

Get yourself a nice bright folder with some colourful dividers, and once completed put all these documents in one place. That way should you ever be asked to show your policies, or if the worst happens and you need to refer to them due to a real-life situation, then you will know where to find them.

It will take you a while to go through them all and complete them with your details. However, when you have done this once you can simply check them on a yearly basis, record that you have looked at them and checked if anything needs to change and refile them.

Here is a list of the most useful (and essential) documents you will need in order to set up your own practice. This list is taken from the IO website, so is fairly comprehensive, but I have added a couple more which I use in my own practice.

If you are working as an associate in an existing practice you will not need to complete these documents yourself, but please check with your principal that they have copies available for you to see. If they don't have them completed it would be a really useful exercise for you to go through them with your principal so you can see how you need to complete them if you ever choose to set up your own practice.

Don't be surprised if your principal doesn't have all these documents completed – more often than not they are just unaware that they need to have them, so your involvement in helping them complete them will (hopefully) be welcome.

Forms necessary to have completed in the practice

- Equality and Diversity
- GDPR
- Safeguarding policy for working with vulnerable adults

- Safeguarding policy for working with children
- Health and Safety Risk Assessment Template
- Health and Safety Policy Template
- Health and safety Policy: Incident report form
- Fire safety policy
- Communicating with GPs
- Infection Control
- Register with Information Commission

The finer details:

Equality and Diversity

> **Equality** is eliminating discrimination and ensuring equal opportunity and access for employees and patients.
>
> **Diversity** can be described as recognising and valuing different backgrounds, knowledge, skills and experiences.

The **Equality Act** became law in October 2010. It replaced previous legislation (such as the Race Relations **Act** 1976 and the Disability Discrimination **Act** 1995) and ensures consistency in what employers and employees need to do to make their workplaces a fair environment and comply with the law. (taken from IO document)

This law also covers those coming into the practice for treatments.

The IO has an 8-page document with all the relevant information for you to fill in for your own practice.

GDPR (General Data Protection Rules) and privacy policy

In May 2018 new data protection rules were introduced in an attempt to stop unsolicited emails and text messages being sent out. Whenever you take information from your patients, you need to have their consent to do so, and they need to be informed about how you are storing their information.

It is necessary to find out how they want you to communicate with them in any future dealings, i.e. text message reminders for their appointments, and if they are happy to receive any marketing information from you, such as newsletters.

You will also need to have in place a 'Privacy Policy' which sets out how you deal with your patients' information and how they can access their files should they want to. This needs to be available for them to read on your website, as well as in your practice. I have to be honest, since 2018 when I put mine in place no one has had any interest in reading it, as it is a very long document, but you never know when that one patient will come in determined to read it cover to cover.

The IO has a great GDPR toolkit, which is ready set up for you to fill in with your own details. You can only access it if you are an IO member, and so my advice is to join the IO and you will get it for free.

Safeguarding for vulnerable adults/children

What is safeguarding and why do I need a policy?

A Safeguarding policy makes it clear what your clinic/organisation will do to ensure that children and vulnerable adults are safe when they come for treatment. It needs to be read and understood by all members of your staff/team as safeguarding is everyone's responsibility.

It is important never to make assumptions about abuse, it can occur in every setting, rich or poor, privileged or not, and so we all need to be aware of this in our dealings with everyone. It is equally important that you and your team know the following:

1. How to recognise symptoms of abuse or neglect
2. Know what to do if you are concerned about a vulnerable person.
3. Maintain the skills and knowledge to protect all patients.

Explaining the above points is outside of the remit of this book, but the IO has a great 16-page document all about this subject so if you are a member go to the *'Policies and Guidance'* section in the 'For Osteopaths' section.

You should have a written policy for both categories, vulnerable adults and children and these should be kept in your policy document folder.

Health & Safety Risk Assessment

People will be coming into your building for treatments. Practitioners will be coming in to look after those people. Employees will be coming in to do their job. All these different people coming into your building need to know that they will be safe to do their work and that the environment isn't hazardous or dangerous to them.

It isn't essential that osteopathic practices with fewer than five employees have a health and safety policy, but it is definitely good practice to have one.

This is the purpose of a health and safety risk assessment, to look around the building and check for hazards which might put people's safety at risk. It is a very important document, because if an incident occurred where someone was injured or hurt, and you didn't have a policy in place your insurers might not be able to cover you properly. If it is just you working on your own you don't necessarily need a very detailed one, but it is important that you have taken the time to look and assess your premises for health and safety hazards.

Again the IO has a great template for you to complete for your own needs.

Fire Safety Policy

I'll let you into a secret – I didn't have one of these in place when my local Fire Officer came round to check what my safety policy was! Rather embarrassing to say the least! However, he did inform me that as I had under five employees it wasn't essential but that it would be very sensible to have one in place, firstly because reducing the risk of a fire occurring makes perfect sense, but also any insurance company might not look favourably on you if you hadn't made some attempt at reducing fire risk.

The IO doesn't have a template for this one, so head over to my website and hit the 'resources' button and you will find a copy of mine there for you to adapt.

Communicating with GPs

The reason for putting this section in comes from writing to GPs over many years and realising that most of the time I was saying the same thing in each letter so why not just set up some templates to make things simpler.

I have a template to go with my patient consent form when writing to GPs for copies of patient notes. Head over to my website and you will find the link there to download your own copy.

Accident Book

What would happen if either a patient or someone who works in the practice has an accident whilst at work? You need to keep records of any accidents or injuries that happen in the workplace, and the best place to store this information is in your policy document.

Infection Control

As we are now living in a Covid-19 world, this is one of the most important documents you need to have in place. For the most up to date information I would suggest going to the IO website, as they are in regular contact with Public Health England and regularly update their information.

Speaking as an osteopath who has worked through COVID-19, patients need to feel safe when they come into your building for treatment. You must ensure that your building looks cared for, clean and tidy. Patients understand the risks of coming in for treatment, but they need to know that you are doing all you can to minimise those risks. Patients often remark to me that my building 'smells clean', and they like the fact that everything is easy to wipe.

Registering with the Information Commission

This isn't a policy document, but it is something that you need to investigate if you process patient records electronically. If you go to the ICO website at www.ico.org.uk there is a quick test you can take to see if you need to pay a fee.

To help make this process easier for you, and to ensure that you have completed all the necessary documents you will find below a table for you to complete, along with dates the forms were completed, and any future dates for the policies to be renewed. There is also a link to one on my website: www.thetherapyrooms.co.uk. > > Survive & Thrive menu > > Enter password S&T2021#New

HMRC

If this is your first-time being self-employed you will need to register with HMRC for tax and national insurance purposes. You need to do this within three months of becoming self-employed. HMRC often has webinars to help you with completing your self-assessment tax form, check out www.gov.uk/hmrc

Table of Required Documents for Setting up your practice

	Name of Document	Date started	Date completed
1	Equality and Diversity		
2	GDPR		
3	Safeguarding – adults		
4	Safeguarding – children		
5	Health and Safety – Risk Assessment		
6	Health and Safety – template		
7	Health and Safety – incident report form		
8	Fire Safety Policy		
9	Communicating with GPs		
10	Infection Control		
11	Accident book		
12	Register with Information Commission		
13	Register with HMRC		

FINAL WORDS

So there you have it – the complete guide on how to be an osteopath! I'm joking of course, but I truly hope that you have found some really useful and constructive information in these pages which will help you to start on your osteopathic journey with a bit more understanding and guidance.

But our relationship doesn't end there – I have more information on my website, with downloadable resources to help you even more.

If you have enjoyed this book then please tell your friends and colleagues about it and encourage them to read it too.

And why not become one of my Survive and Thrive founding members – head over to my website for more details of how to join and what benefits you will receive.

So go out, build your business, enjoy your work, look after your patients with care and understanding and be the best osteopath you can be!

And what better way to finish than with some words from Andrew Taylor Still, taken from 'Osteopathy Research and Practice'

'Osteopathy is based on the perfection of Nature's work. When all parts of the human body are in line we have health.'

REFERENCES

Miller, Jennie. *Boundaries: How to Draw the Line in Your Head, Heart and Home*. HQ, 2018.

Still, T., A. *Osteopathy Research and Practice.* Independently Published, 2017.

Suggested Reading

Lewis, R., *J. A. T. Still: From the Dry Bone to the Living Man*. Dry Bone Press, 2012.

Woodhouse, G. *Osteobiz Guide to Fearless Marketing: Easy Ideas to Increase Patient Bookings!*. Independently Published, 2019.

ABOUT THE AUTHOR

Elizabeth Curphey was born and raised in Cheshire and now lives in Macclesfield, a thriving town in the foothills of the Peak District from where she runs her multi-disciplinary practice. She loves treating patients of all ages, but has a particular interest in working with babies and children. She is also a Master Practitioner in NLP and Time Line Therapy®.

Since qualifying as an osteopath over 20 years ago her passion has been to do more for her patients than they would ever expect, and has built up an excellent reputation in her local community as a caring and compassionate practitioner.

When not at work you are most likely to find her enjoying long walks in the beautiful Cheshire countryside with her family, or in her kitchen trying out some new cake recipes.

Printed in Great Britain
by Amazon